American Language Hub

CB081755

LEVEL 1A
Student's Book

PETER MAGGS
CATHERINE SMITH

macmillan education

Contents

1 ARRIVALS

A traveler watching the sun rise over a new city.

OBJECTIVES

- talk about countries and nationalities
- ask and answer questions about a place
- talk about everyday items
- greet people and make introductions
- fill in a form with personal details

Work with a partner. Discuss the questions.

1 Where are you from?
2 Look at the picture. Which country is this?
3 What's your favorite city?

1.1 People and places

Talk about countries and nationalities

V countries and nationalities P syllable stress G simple present *be*: positive and negative

LISTENING

1.1 **A LISTEN FOR GIST** Look at the picture and listen. Are the two women friends?

1.1 **B LISTEN FOR DETAIL** Choose the correct options to complete the boarding pass. Then listen again and check.

1.1 **C LISTEN FOR KEY WORDS** Listen again. Choose the correct words to complete the sentences.

Canadian Mexico Mexico City names

1 Helen likes Spanish ________________.
2 Veronica is from ________________.
3 Helen is ________________.
4 Helen's company is in ________________.

D SPEAK Work in pairs. Introduce yourself to your partner.

A: Hi. I'm Anton.
B: Nice to meet you, Anton. I'm Katie.

VOCABULARY
Countries and nationalities

A Work in pairs. Look at the flight map. Match the numbers on the screen (1–4) with the countries in the box.

___ Brazil ___ Canada ___ Mexico ___ the US

B Go to the **Vocabulary Hub** on **page XVIII**.

PRONUNCIATION
Syllable stress

1.2 **A** A syllable is a word or a part of a word that has only one vowel sound. Listen and repeat the words.

One syllable words	Two-syllable words	Three-syllable words	Four-syllable words
France	*Japan*	*Canada*	*Canadian*
French	*China*	*Mexico*	
	Chinese	*Mexican*	
		Japanese	

1.3 **B** Add the words in the box to the table in Exercise A. Then listen, check and repeat.

Brazil American India Indian Spain Spanish

C Underline the stressed syllables in the table in Exercise A. Use the information box to help you.

Syllable stress
In words with multiple syllables, one syllable is stressed more than others.
●● Ja<u>pan</u> ●● <u>Chi</u>na ●●● <u>In</u>dian

GRAMMAR

Simple present *be*: positive and negative

1.1 **A** Listen to the conversation between Helen and Veronica again. Complete the conversation with *'m*, *'s* or *'m not*.

Helen: Excuse me, is this row 15?

Veronica: Yes. I'm in seat 15A.

Helen: My seat is 15B. Hi, I [1] _______________ Helen.

Veronica: Nice to meet you. I'm Veronica Martinez.

Helen: That [2] _______________ a nice name. I like Spanish names.

Veronica: Thanks, but I [3] _______________ Spanish. I'm Mexican. I'm from Mexico. Where are you from?

Helen: I [4] _______________ Canadian, but I live in Mexico. My company's office is in Mexico City.

Pilot: Good morning, ladies and gentlemen. This is the 9:45 flight to Mexico City …

B WORK IT OUT Choose the correct options to complete the rules. Use the conversation in Exercise A to help you.

Simple present *be*

1. We use *'m*, *'s* and *'re* to make ***positive*** / ***negative*** sentences with *be*.
2. We use *'m not*, *isn't* and *aren't* to make ***positive*** / ***negative*** sentences with *be*.

C Go to the **Grammar Hub** on **page VI**.

1.4 **D** Listen to Chloe introducing herself. Complete the introduction with the correct forms of *be*.

Hi, I [1] _______________ Chloe.
I [2] _______________ from France.
I often go to Germany to see my friend, Camille. We [3] _______________ old friends.
Camille lives in Berlin, but she [4] _______________ German.
She [5] _______________ French like me. Her boyfriend,
Luc [6] _______________ German, but his mother and father [7] _______________.
They [8] _______________ French.

E Write three sentences about nationality – two true, and one false.

I'm Japanese. I'm not Chinese. My mother is Japanese.

F SPEAK Work in pairs. Read your sentences from Exercise E. Guess which sentence is false.

A: I'm Japanese. I'm not Chinese. My mother is Japanese.
B: You're Japanese. That's true. But your mother isn't Japanese. She's French!

SPEAKING

A THINK Imagine you are on an airplane. Choose the country you are from.

B PLAN You are going to introduce yourself to another passenger. Look at the model conversation and write notes on what you are going to say.

A: Hello, is this seat 14B?
B: Yes, it is. I'm in seat 14A. Hi, I'm Frederic by the way.
A: Nice to meet you, Frederic. I'm Sonia. I'm from Italy.
B: Nice to meet you, too, Sonia! I live in Italy, too. But I'm French. My wife is Italian.
A: Oh, great! I'm Italian, but my family isn't. They're Spanish.

C SPEAK Work in pairs. Practice your conversation.

Talk about countries and nationalities

1.2 Where are you?

Ask and answer questions about a place

V big numbers P similar numbers G simple present *be*: questions

READING

A Work with a partner. Look at the picture in the text message below. Where is it?

Carlos
Typing ...

Hi Carlos! Where am I?

Hi Lee. I don't know. Where are you?

I'm 6,028 miles from home – that's 13 hours by plane.

🙁

I'm in Japan! It's amazing 😊. The picture is from my hotel window. There are thousands of people everywhere. It's always busy.

Wow! Where are you in Japan? Is the food good? Is it hot there? Tell me more!!!

I'm in Tokyo. Yes, the food is really good. There are hundreds of great restaurants 😉 Is it hot here? 😂 It's very HOT 🌡. It's 30 degrees every day ☹. How are you? Is work busy?

I'm fine. Work isn't busy – everyone is on vacation ☹. Except me!

B READ FOR GIST Read the messages between Carlos and Lee. Where is Lee?

C READ FOR DETAIL Read again. Are the sentences true (T) or false (F)? Correct the false sentences.

1 Japan is far from where Carlos and Lee live. *T / F*
2 The picture is from Carlos's work. *T / F*
3 It isn't hot where Lee is. *T / F*
4 Lee likes Japanese food. *T / F*
5 Carlos is very busy at work. *T / F*

VOCABULARY

Big numbers

A Match numbers (1–5) with the words (a–e).

1 100	**a** one million
2 1,000	**b** ten thousand
3 10,000	**c** one hundred thousand
4 100,000	**d** one thousand
5 1,000,000	**e** one hundred

1.5 **B** Listen and write the numbers you hear.

1 ____________
2 ____________
3 ____________

C SPEAK Work in pairs. How far is Lee from home?

D SPEAK Work in pairs. Student A – say how far a city is from Paris. Student B – name the city. Then swap.

Paris → New York	3,625 miles
Paris → Melbourne	10,427 miles
Paris → Seoul	5,568 miles
Paris → Milan	529 miles
Paris → Cape Town	7,965 miles

A: This city is 5,568 miles from Paris.
B: It's Seoul. This city is ...

PRONUNCIATION

Similar numbers

1.6 **A** Listen to part of a phone call between Carlos and Lee. Which number does Lee say?

a thirteen (13)
b thirty (30)

1.7 **B** Listen and repeat. Underline the stressed syllables in the numbers in Exercise A.

1.8 **C** Listen and check (✓) the number you hear.

a	17 ☐	70 ☐	**e**	16 ☐	60 ☐
b	19 ☐	90 ☐	**f**	14 ☐	40 ☐
c	15 ☐	50 ☐	**g**	18 ☐	80 ☐
d	12 ☐	20 ☐	**h**	13 ☐	30 ☐

1.8 **D** Listen again and repeat the numbers.

GRAMMAR

Simple present *be*: questions

A WORK IT OUT Look at the text conversation between Lee and Carlos again. Complete the table with words from the text.

Wh- questions	*Yes/No* questions
A: Where [1]________ you? **B:** I [2]________ in Tokyo.	**A:** [5]________ the food good? **B:** Yes, the food [6]________ really good.
A: How [3]________ you? **B:** I [4]________ fine.	**A:** [7]________ it hot there? **B:** It [8]________ very hot.

B Look at the table in Exercise A and complete the rules.

Present simple *be*: questions

1 We put question words ***before* / *after*** *be*.
2 We put the subject ***before* / *after*** *be*.
3 When we answer *yes/no* questions, we put the subject ***before* / *after*** *be*.

C Go to the **Grammar Hub** on **page VI**.

D PRACTICE Match the questions (1–5) with the answers (a–e).

1 Where are you?
2 How far is Mumbai from there?
3 Is your city big?
4 Are you Egyptian?
5 What's your flight number?

a It's 10 hours by plane.
b It's J230.
c No, I'm not.
d Yes, it is.
e I'm at the hotel.

E SPEAK Work in pairs. Write questions, adding the correct form of *be*. Take turns asking and answering questions.

1 Where / from? ____________________
2 food good / your country? ____________________
3 your hometown / big? ____________________
4 your hometown / hot or cold? ____________________
5 How far / your home / from here? ____________________

LISTENING

A LISTEN FOR GIST Listen to Carlos and Lee talking on the phone. Where is Lee now? 1.9

B LISTEN FOR DETAIL Listen again. Number Carlos's questions in the order you hear them (1–6). 1.9

___ Are you still in Tokyo?
___ Is the food good?
___ What's it like there?
___ What's your next destination?
___ Where are you in China?
_1_ Where are you?

C Work in pairs. Answer the questions in Exercise B for Lee.

SPEAKING

A PREPARE Choose a place. It could be your home or another place that you know. Imagine you are in that place. What is it like? Think about:

- far from here?
- busy/quiet?
- hot/cold at the moment?
- what kind of food?

B PLAN Use the prompts in Exercise A to make questions to ask your partner about the place he/she is in.

C SPEAK Work in pairs. Take turns asking and answering questions about your places. Guess where the place is.

Ask and answer questions about a place

V– everyday items G– *a/an* and plural nouns; *this, that, these, those* P– vowel sounds: /ɪ/ /æ/ /iː/ /oʊ/ S– reading for gist

What's in your **carry-on bag?**

Three travel experts talk about the things in their carry-on bag when they go on a plane.

Bruce I don't carry a lot of luggage when I go on a plane. My bag is very small. **I have a bottle of water and tissues.** That's it. I buy the water at the airport once I am through security. I usually sleep on a plane.

Wei I never use a suitcase. I put everything in my carry-on bag, so there's no need to wait at baggage claim. My carry-on bag is very heavy, but that's OK. **I have two watches.** I wear one and I put one in my bag, so I always know what time it is at home. **I travel to lots of countries.** I just want to get off the plane and leave the airport as soon as I can.

Elif I always have a laptop and my phone in my carry-on bag when I go on a plane. **I usually have an umbrella and my keys.** Flying is a good time to do my work. I can relax at home.

VOCABULARY
Everyday items

A Work in pairs. Look at the picture. Match the items in the picture (1–12) with the words in the box.

___ a bottle of water	___ a credit card
___ headphones ___ keys	___ a laptop
___ a magazine	___ a cell phone
___ a bag ___ tissues	___ an umbrella
___ a wallet	___ a watch

B SPEAK Work in pairs. Tell your partner what is in your bag.

A: What's in your bag?
B: My keys, a bottle of water and an umbrella.

READING

A READ FOR GIST Read *What's in your carry-on bag?* What is the text about? Things people …

a take to work.
b take to a party.
c take on a plane.

Reading for gist

When you read a text for the first time, it is important to get a general idea of what it is about. Think about:

- the title of the text and the pictures
- the general topic
- key words

B READ FOR DETAIL Read the text again. Are these sentences true (T) or false (F)? Correct the false sentences.

1 Bruce's bag is very big. *T / F*
2 Bruce takes a bottle of water and tissues on the plane. *T / F*
3 Wei never uses a suitcase. *T / F*
4 Wei always has his watch and a wallet in his bag. *T / F*
5 Elif likes to relax on the plane. *T / F*

GRAMMAR
a/an and plural nouns

A WORK IT OUT Look at the bold sentences in *What's in your carry-on bag?* Underline the nouns in each sentence.

B Look at the nouns you highlighted in Exercise A and complete the rules.

***a/an* and plural nouns**

1 We use *a/an* with ***plural* / *singular*** nouns.
2 We use *a* with singular nouns that begin with a ***consonant sound* / *vowel sound***.
3 We use *an* with singular nouns that begin with a ***consonant sound* / *vowel sound***.
4 We add **-*s*** / **-*es*** to most nouns to make a plural.
5 We add **-*s*** / **-*es*** to nouns that end in -*s* or -*ch* to make a plural.
6 For nouns that end in consonant + -*y*, we cut the -*y* and add **-*es*** / **-*ies***.

C Go to the Grammar Hub on page VI.

D SPEAK Work in pairs. Point to items in the picture in Vocabulary Exercise A. Your partner says what it is.

Welcome

GREETINGS

A 0.1 Read and listen to three conversations. Match conversations (1–3) with pictures (a–c).

a b c

1 ___

Marc: Hi, Luca.
Luca: Hi, Marc. How are you?
Marc: Fine, thanks.

2 ___

Emily: Good morning.
David: Hello. Nice to meet you.
Emily: You, too.

3 ___

Gudrun: Bye, Clara.
Clara: Bye, Gudrun. See you later.

B Complete the table with the words and phrases in the box.

~~Bye.~~ ~~Fine, thanks.~~ ~~Good afternoon.~~ ~~How are you?~~ Good morning. Goodbye. Hi. Good night. I'm very well, thank you. Good evening. Not too bad. See you later.

Say hello	Ask a question	Answer	Say goodbye
Good afternoon.	*How are you?*	*Fine, thanks.*	*Bye.*

C Complete the conversations with words from Exercise B.

1 A: How are you? B: Not too ______________.
2 A: Goodbye. B: ______________ night.
3 A: How are you? B: I'm very ______________, thanks.
4 A: Bye. B: ______________ you later.

NUMBERS 0–100

A 0.2 Listen and repeat the numbers.

0 1 2 3 4 5 6 7 8 9 10 11 12 13 14 15 16 17 18 19 20 21
30 40 50 60 70 80 90 100

B 0.3 Listen and write the numbers you hear.

a ___ c ___ e ___ g ___
b ___ d ___ f ___ h ___

DAYS OF THE WEEK

0.4 Write the days of the week in the correct order. Then listen and repeat.

Friday ~~Monday~~ Saturday Sunday Thursday Tuesday Wednesday

1 *Monday*
2 ______________
3 ______________
4 ______________
5 ______________
6 ______________
7 ______________

THE ALPHABET

A 0.5 Listen and repeat the letters of the alphabet.

a b c d e f g h i j k l m n o p q r s t u v w x y z

B 0.6 Circle the letter in each group that has a different sound. Then listen and check.

1 b g (m) 2 a f k 3 j i y 4 l m r 5 i e t

C 0.7 Listen and write the colors.

1 ______________
2 ______________
3 ______________
4 ______________
5 ______________
6 ______________

D SPEAK Work in pairs. Spell these things for your partner to write.

- your first name
- your last name

CLASSROOM INSTRUCTIONS

0.8 Match questions (1–5) with replies (a–e). Then listen and check.

1 What does *book* mean?
2 What's *libro* in English?
3 I don't understand.
4 Could you repeat that, please?
5 Could you write it down, please?

a That's OK. I'll explain it again.
b Yes, sure.
c It means *libro*.
d It's *book*.
e Of course – *book*.

LISTENING

A SPEAK Work in pairs. Which of these items can you take in your carry-on bag?

B LISTEN FOR GIST Listen to two conversations at airport security. Which items from Exercise A does:

1.10

1 the woman have in her bag?

2 the man have in his bag?

C LISTEN FOR KEY WORDS Listen again. Complete the sentences with the correct words.

1.10

1 **A:** Excuse me, ma'am. Is this your __________?
B: Yes, it is.

2 **A:** OK. You can go. Oh, wait! Are these your __________?
B: Oh, yes, they are! Thank you so much!

3 **A:** Excuse me, sir. Is that your __________?
B: Yes, it is.

4 **A:** Are those your __________?
B: No, they aren't. I think they belong to that family over there.

PRONUNCIATION

Vowel sounds: /ɪ/ /æ/ /iː/ /oʊ/

A Listen carefully and notice the vowel sounds. Then listen again and repeat.

1.11

/ɪ/ this, kiss, sit /iː/ these, key, tree

/æ/ that, hat, cat /oʊ/ those, toes, nose

B SPEAK Work in pairs. Practice the conversations in Listening Exercise C.

GRAMMAR

this, that, these, those

A WORK IT OUT Look at the pictures. Match the situations (1–4) from Listening Exercise C with the pictures (a–d).

B Choose the correct words to complete the rules.

this, that, these, those

1 We use *this / that* to talk about a singular noun that's near.

2 We use *this / that* to talk about a singular noun that isn't near.

3 We use *these / those* to talk about a plural noun that is near.

4 We use *these / those* to talk about a plural noun that isn't near.

C Go to the **Grammar Hub** on **page VI**.

SPEAKING HUB

A Work in pairs. Imagine you are going on vacation. Draw six everyday items to take with you.

B PLAN Work alone. Choose three of the items in Exercise A to take in your carry-on bag.

C DISCUSS Imagine you are at airport security. Try to find out what is in your partner's carry-on bag. Follow these steps:

Student A – Point to a picture in Exercise A and ask a question with *Is this / Are these your …?*

Student B – Answer Student A's question.

Student A – Keep asking questions until you know which three items are in your partner's bag.

Talk about everyday items

Café Hub

1.4 Good morning

F – greet people and make introductions **P** – word stress

COMPREHENSION

A ▶ Watch the video. Complete the information about each person in the photo captions below.

B Write a question about each person in Exercise A.

1 How old is Sam?

2 Where is Gaby from?

3 Is Milly married?

C SPEAK Work in pairs. Close your books and ask each other your question from Exercise B.

A: How old is Sam?

B: He's 34.

FUNCTIONAL LANGUAGE

Greeting people and making introductions

A Complete the phrases with the words in the box.

bad fine ~~Hi~~ meet morning See too you

Say hello	Greet people + reply
Hello.	How are you?
1 ___*Hi*___.	Not too 3 ___.
Hey!	I'm 4 ___, thanks.
Good 2 ___.	Very well, thanks.
Good afternoon.	
Good evening.	

Introduce people + reply	Say goodbye
This is …	Bye.
This is my friend …	See 7 ___.
It's nice to 5 ___ you.	See you soon.
Nice to meet you, 6 ___.	8 ___ you later.

B ▶ Watch the first part of the video again. Check your answers to Exercise A.

Glossary

flat **(n) (British)** = apartment **(n) (American)**

pounds **(n) (British)** = dollars **(n) (American)**

MILLY

SAM

NEENA

ZAC

GABY

USEFUL PHRASES

A Match the useful phrases (1–3) with the replies (a–c).

1 What would you like?
2 That's £2, please.
3 Take a seat.

a Thanks.
b Can I have a croissant to go, please?
c Here you go.

B 00:24–01:14 Watch part of the video again and check your answers to Exercise A.

PRONUNCIATION

Word stress

A 00:24–01:14 Watch part of the video again and read the conversation. Notice that the underlined words are stressed.

Neena: Good morning. How are you Sam?
Sam: Not too bad. How are you?
Neena: I'm fine, thanks. This is my friend, Milly.
Sam: Hi Milly. Nice to meet you.
Milly: Nice to meet you, too.

B 00:24–01:14 Watch again and repeat the conversation. Copy the word stress.

C **SPEAK** Work in groups of three. Practice the conversation in Exercise A. Remember to use the correct stress.

SPEAKING

A **PREPARE** Walk around the class. Introduce yourself to your classmates.

A: Hello, I'm Andreas. It's nice to meet you.
B: It's nice to meet you, too.

B **DISCUSS** Work in pairs. Walk around the class. Greet the people you know and introduce your partner.

A: Hello, I'm Andreas. It's nice to meet you.
B: It's nice to meet you, too.
A: This is Nadia.

C **PLAN** You're going to record a 'selfie' presentation. Write notes about what you want to say. Then record it.

Introducing	
Hi! My name's …	I'm …
My friends call me …	I'm from …
I'm single/married …	I'm a …

D **PRESENT** Work in groups. Compare your presentations.

Greet people and make introductions

➤ Turn to page XXIV to learn how to fill in a form with personal details.

Unit 1 Review

VOCABULARY

A Complete the table with the correct countries and nationalities.

Country	Nationality
Brazil	1 ________
2 ________	Chinese
3 ________	Egyptian
India	4 ________
Japan	5 ________
6 ________	Portuguese
Sweden	7 ________
The UK	8 ________

B Correct the mistakes in each sentence.

1 Tokyo is the capital of Japanese.
2 IKEA is a Sweden company.
3 My father's from Hanoi in Vietnamese.
4 I'm from New York, in US.
5 I love Switzerland chocolate!

C Match the words (1–8) with the numbers (a–h).

1 one million — **a** 500,000
2 five hundred and ten — **b** 510
3 fifty-five thousand — **c** 5,002
4 one thousand two hundred — **d** 1,000,000
5 five hundred thousand — **e** 1,200
6 one hundred thousand — **f** 55,000
7 five thousand and two — **g** 250
8 two hundred and fifty — **h** 100,000

D Complete the everyday items with *a, e, i, o* or *u*.

1 h_e_a_dph_o_n_e_s
2 a cr__d__t c__rd
3 m__n__y
4 a c__ll ph__n__
5 a b__ttl__ of w__t__r
6 a w__tch
7 a b__x of t__ss__ __s
8 a l__pt__p
9 a m__g__z__n__
10 a w__ll__t

E SPEAK Work in pairs. Discuss the questions.

1 Where are you from?
2 How old are you?
3 What nationality are your parents?
4 What's the capital of your country?
5 What's in your bag?

GRAMMAR

A Choose the correct words to complete the sentences.

1 I *'m / 's* from the US.
2 We *'s / 're* Russian.
3 They *isn't / aren't* married.
4 You *'s / 're* my friend.
5 She *isn't / aren't* American.
6 He *'m / 's* 36 years old.
7 I *isn't / 'm not* from Sweden.

B Write questions and short answers.

1 you / Japanese
Are you Japanese (?) _Yes, I am._ (+)
2 they / students
________ (?) ________ (+)
3 he / German
________ (?) ________ (-)
4 she / 18 years old
________ (?) ________ (+)
5 you / married
________ (?) ________ (-)

C Match the questions (1–4) with the answers (a–d).

1 What's your name? — **a** Oakland.
2 How old are you? — **b** It's in the US.
3 Where are you from? — **c** Susan.
4 Where's that? — **d** 26.

D Complete the text with *a, an* or – (no article).

This is my bag. I usually carry 1 ________ apple, 2 ________ cell phone and 3 ________ keys. Oh, and 4 ________ credit card!

E Choose the correct words to complete the sentences.

1 Is *this / these* your phone?
2 *That / Those* aren't my keys.
3 *That / Those* 's my book.
4 Are *this / these* your sunglasses?

FUNCTIONAL LANGUAGE

A Complete the conversation with the words in the box.

from Good Hi meet small Where

A: 1 ________. I'm Andreas.
B: Nice to 2 ________ you, Andreas. I'm Tia.
A: 3 ________ to meet you, too, Tia.
B: 4 ________ are you from, Andreas?
A: Switzerland. I live in a 5 ________ town near Zurich.
B: Really? I'm 6 ________ Chicago, but I live in Paris.

B Work in pairs. Practice the conversation in Exercise A. Use your own information.

2 PEOPLE

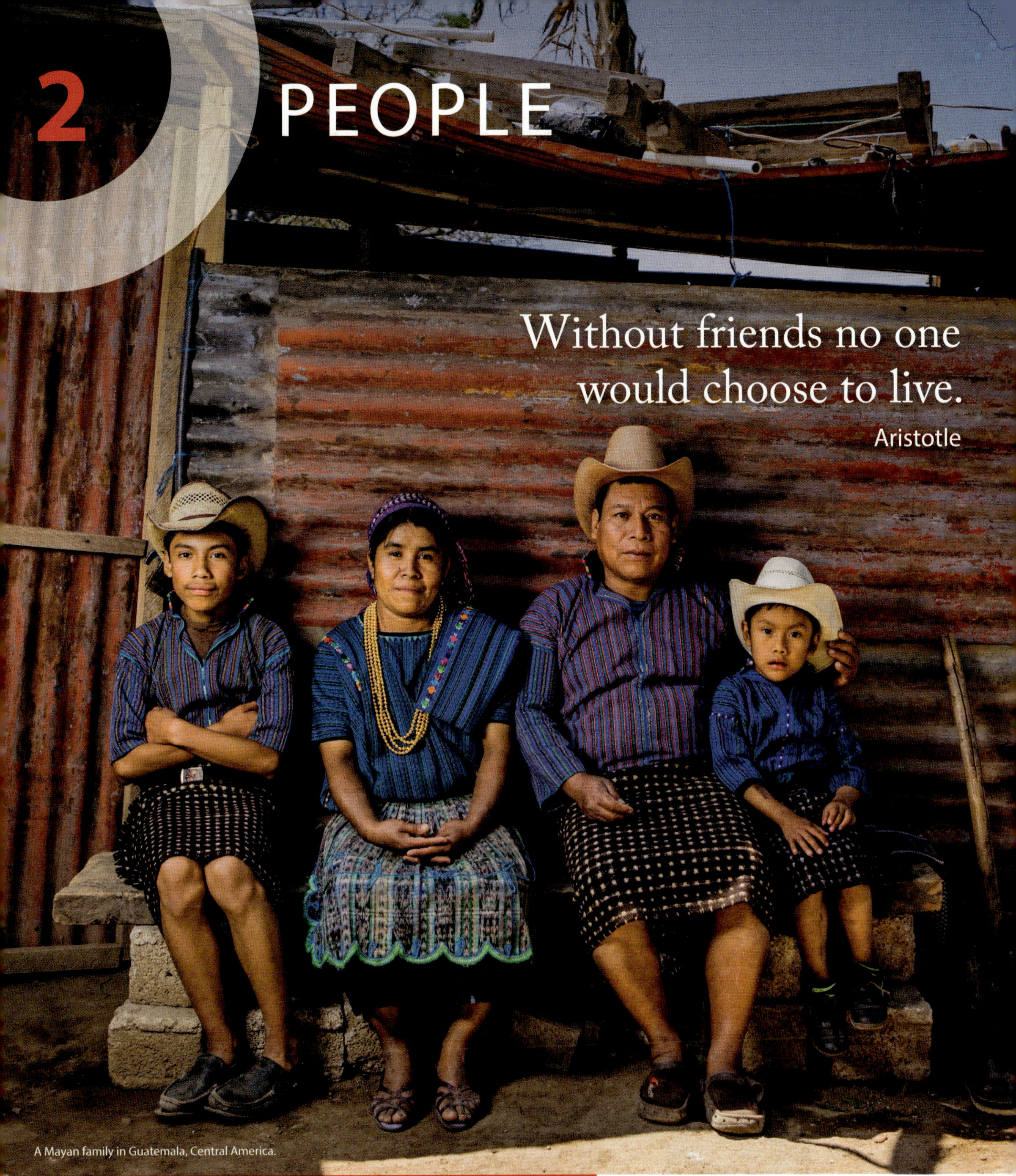

Without friends no one would choose to live.

Aristotle

A Mayan family in Guatemala, Central America.

OBJECTIVES

- talk about your family
- talk about appearance
- describe family members and friends
- make and respond to requests
- write an email to a friend

Work with a partner. Discuss the questions.

1 Do you have a big family?

2 Do you have any brothers or sisters?

3 What do you like doing with your friends?

2.1 Family

Talk about your family

V family **P** /ə/ 'schwa' **G** possessive adjectives and apostrophes

READING

A Work in pairs. Look at the pictures in *Famous Families.* Why are these people famous?

B **READ FOR GIST** Read *Famous Families* and check your answers to Exercise A.

C Work in pairs. How many of the people do you know?

D **READ FOR DETAIL** Read *Famous Families* again. Are the sentences true (T) or false (F)? Correct the false sentences.

1 Sofia is a famous actress. T / F
2 Sofia's grandparents were Italian. T / F
3 Sofia's brother is named Francis Ford Coppola. T / F
4 Sofia's aunt was in the movie *Rocky*. T / F
5 Sofia and her husband, Thomas, live in Italy. T / F

E **SPEAK** Work in pairs. What other famous families do you know?

FAMOUS FAMILIES

This week, we continue our series on Hollywood families with a look at the Coppolas.

Sofia Coppola is an American screenwriter and director. She's famous for directing the movies *Marie Antoinette*, *Somewhere, The Bling Ring* and *The Beguiled*. Sofia's family is famous, too. There are famous movie directors, actors and musicians in her family.

Her grandparents, Carmine Coppola and Italia Pennino, were musicians from Italy. Sofia's father is the movie director Francis Ford Coppola. He is the director of the three *Godfather* movies. Sofia's brother, Roman Coppola, is also a movie director.

Sofia's aunt is Talia Shire. She's an actress, and she was in the *Godfather* and the *Rocky* movies. Talia's son is the actor Jason Schwartzman. Jason is Sofia's cousin. The actor Nicolas Cage is her cousin, too. Nicolas's father was August Coppola. He was Francis Ford Coppola's brother.

Sofia's husband is Thomas Mars, the singer of the rock band Phoenix. Sofia and Thomas live in New York City, and they have two daughters. Their daughters' names are Romy Mars and Cosima Mars.

Thomas Mars

Sofia Coppola

Francis Ford Coppola

Talia Shire

Jason Schwartzman

VOCABULARY

Family

A Look at the word in **bold** in the sentence below. Find and underline seven other words for family members in *Famous families*.

*Her **grandparents**, Carmine Coppola and Italia Pennino, were musicians.*

B Read the text again. Complete the family tree.

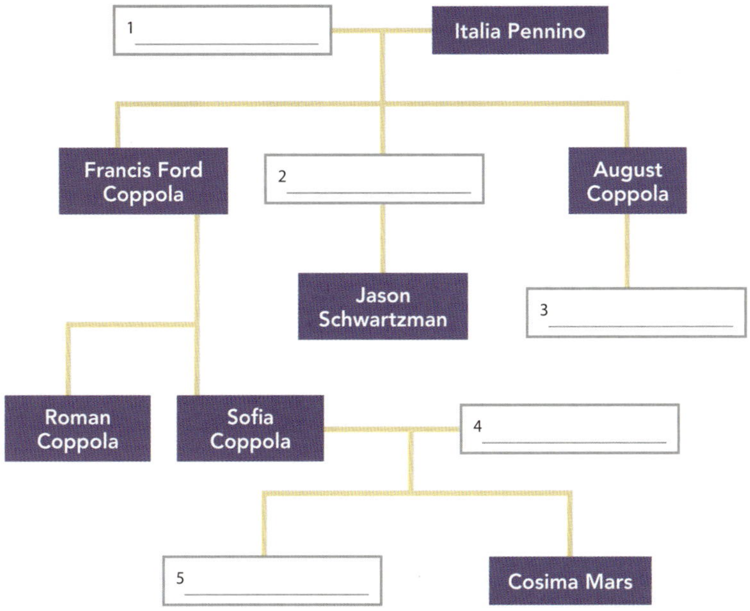

C Complete the table with the words you found in Exercise A.

Female	Male	Female or male
		grandparents

D Add the words in the box to the table in Exercise C.

children grandfather grandmother mother parents sister uncle wife

E **SPEAK** Work in pairs. Student A – go to the **Communication Hub** on **page XXI**. Student B – go to the **Communication Hub** on **page XXII**.

PRONUNCIATION

/ə/ 'schwa'

2.1 **A** Listen and repeat. Notice how we say the underlined sounds.

/ə/ family, husband, famous

2.2 **B** Say these words with a partner. Underline the /ə/ sound in each word. Then listen, check and repeat.

actress family famous husband parents sister television woman

GRAMMAR

Possessive adjectives and apostrophes

A Look at the sentences from *Famous families*. Which name matches the word in **bold**? Choose a, b or c.

1 *Jason is Sofia's cousin. The actor Nicolas Cage is **her** cousin, too.*
  a Jason b Sofia c Nicolas

2 *Sofia and Thomas live in New York City, and they have two daughters. **Their** daughters' names are Romy Mars and Cosima Mars.*
  a Sofia and Thomas b Sofia c Thomas

B **WORK IT OUT** Complete the table with the words in the box.

his its my our your

Subject pronouns	Possessive adjectives
I	1 ________
you	2 ________
we	3 ________
they	their
he	4 ________
she	her
it	5 ________

C **WORK IT OUT** Look at the underlined words in Exercise A. Then complete the rules.

Possessive apostrophe

1 We add '/'s to regular singular nouns.
2 We add '/'s to regular plural nouns.
3 We use the possessive apostrophe to show that something *belongs to / doesn't belong to* someone.
4 We add *'s* to show that something *belongs to / doesn't belong to someone* when their name ends with an s.

D Go to the **Grammar Hub** on **page VIII**.

SPEAKING

A **PREPARE** Draw your family tree. Include any grandparents, uncles, aunts or cousins.

B **SPEAK** Work with a partner. Take turns telling each other about the people in your family tree.

My grandfather's name is Hiroyuki. He's 98 years old. My grandmother's name is Saya. She's ...

2.2 The same, but different

Talk about appearance

V describing appearance **G** *have/has* **P** *have/has*

1

2

VOCABULARY

Describing appearance

A Work in pairs. Match the people in the pictures (1–2) with the words in the box.

beard	blond hair	blue eyes	brown eyes	curly hair
gray hair	light skin	long hair	short hair	straight hair

B Go to the **Vocabulary Hub** on **page XVIII**.

TWO in a million

This is a picture of Bobby and Riley George on the day they were born. They're twins. They have curly hair, brown eyes and light skin.

a

This is Bobby and Riley three years later, and they look really different! Bobby looks like his mother. He has light skin, blond hair and blue eyes. Riley looks like his father. He has dark skin and brown eyes, and short, brown hair. The boys don't look the same, but do they have the same personality? No, they don't. Bobby is very noisy and Riley is quiet. They really are one in a million!

b

READING

A Look at picture a in *Two in a million*. Choose three sentences that describe the babies.

1 They are the same age.
2 They look different.
3 They look like each other.
4 They have the same parents.
5 They have different parents.

B **READ FOR GIST** Read *Two in a million*. Check your answers to Exercise A. What is the name of the child on the left in picture b?

C **READ FOR DETAIL** Read again. Choose the correct words to complete the sentences.

1 Bobby and Riley's birthdays are on ***the same day* / *different days***.
2 Bobby and Riley look ***the same* / *different*** three years later.
3 Bobby and the twins' mother have ***the same* / *different*** skin color.
4 Riley and Bobby have ***the same* / *different*** personalities.

look like

The phrase *look like* means have the same appearance.

- I/You/We/They + *look like* + noun
  I look like my mother. I don't look like my father.
- He/She It + *looks like* + noun
  My sister doesn't look like me. She looks like our mom.

D **SPEAK** Work in pairs. Describe someone in your class to your partner. Can they guess who it is?

A: He's tall. He has long, brown hair and brown eyes. He looks a little like Johnny Depp ...
B: Is it Matteo?

GRAMMAR

have/has

A WORK IT OUT Look at *Two in a million* again. Complete the sentences with no more than three words from the text.

1 ____________________ brown hair, brown eyes and dark skin.

2 ____________________ blond hair and blue eyes.

3 The boys don't look the same, but do they have the same personality? No, ____________________.

B WORK IT OUT Complete the table with the words from the box.

have have doesn't

	Positive (+) / Negative (-)		
1	I	________ / don't have	blue eyes.
2	He/She/It	has / ________ have	
3	You/They/We	have / don't ________	

C Go to the **Grammar Hub** on **page VIII**.

D PRACTICE Look at the picture. Complete the conversation about the woman with the correct form of *have/has* and *does/does not*. Use contractions.

A: Who do you look like?

B: My aunt. She's my dad's sister.

A: Does your aunt [1] ________ long hair?

B: No, she [2] ________.
She [3] ________ short, gray hair.

A: [4] ________ she [5] ________ glasses?

B: Yes, she [6] ________.

A: What color eyes [7] ________ she have?

B: She [8] ________ blue eyes. We also have the same nose.

E SPEAK Find out who your partner looks like in their family.

I look like my mother. She has brown eyes, like me. And we both have curly hair.

PRONUNCIATION

have/has

2.3 **A** Listen and repeat the phrases with *have* and *has*. Notice the /v/ and /z/ sounds.

2.4 **B** Listen and choose the correct sound /v/ or /z/.

1 he has /v/ /z/
2 it has /v/ /z/
3 I have /v/ /z/
4 she has /v/ /z/
5 they have /v/ /z/
6 you have /v/ /z/

C SPEAK Work in pairs. Complete the sentences about people in your class.

1 I have …
2 You have …
3 He/She has …
4 We have …
5 They have …

LISTENING

A Work in pairs. Describe the man in the picture.

2.5 **B LISTEN FOR KEY WORDS** Listen to a description of the man in Exercise A. Does it match yours?

C SPEAK Work in pairs. Think of someone in your family. Tell your partner how you and this person are the same, and how you are different.

A: My dad doesn't look like me. He has gray hair and a beard. I have brown hair. I have glasses, but he doesn't.

B: My sister looks the same as me. We're twins!

SPEAKING

Work in pairs. Go to the **Communication Hub** on **page XXI**.

Talk about appearance

2.3 Friends

Describe family members and friends

V personality adjectives P syllable stress: adjectives G using adjectives S reading for organization

VOCABULARY

Personality adjectives

A Complete the descriptions with the adjectives in the box.

friendly funny quiet sad neat

1 She's really ____________ – she always makes me laugh.
2 My uncle is a ____________ person. He doesn't talk much; he just listens.
3 Hakim always puts things away after he uses them – he's very ____________.
4 My father's often ____________. He doesn't laugh or smile a lot anymore.
5 Reema is a very nice person – she's ____________ to everyone.

B Match the adjectives (1–5) with their opposites (a–e).

1 friendly	a messy
2 funny	b unfriendly
3 quiet	c happy
4 sad	d noisy
5 neat	e serious

PRONUNCIATION

Syllable stress: adjectives

2.6 Work with a partner. Say the adjectives, and then add them to the table. Listen and check your answers.

~~friendly~~ funny happy messy noisy quiet sad serious neat unfriendly

●	●•	●••	•●•
	friendly		

LISTENING

A 2.7 **LISTEN FOR GIST** Listen to the conversation. Match people (1–3) to the names below.

Zoe _____ Alice _____ Jody _____

B 2.7 **LISTEN FOR DETAIL** Look at the questions and check (✓) the correct person or people. Listen again and check your answers.

	Keisha (speaker)	Zoe	Alice	Jody
1 Who's in the same study group?				
2 Who's funny?				
3 Who's neat?				
4 Who's quiet?				
5 Who's serious?				
6 Who's messy?				

C **SPEAK** Work in pairs. Are you like Keisha, Zoe, Alice or Jody? Give examples.

GRAMMAR

Using adjectives

A **WORK IT OUT** Look at the sentences from the conversation. Underline the adjectives.

1 They're all really friendly.
2 She's a very funny person.
3 She's fairly quiet, but I like her.

B Choose the correct words to complete the rules. Use the sentences in Exercise A to help you.

Using adjectives

1 We put adjectives ***before*** / ***after*** the verb *be*.
2 We put adjectives ***before*** / ***after*** nouns.

C Go to the **Grammar Hub** on **page VIII**.

D **SPEAK** Work with a partner. Tell them about someone you know. Use *really*, *very* or *fairly* in your descriptions.

READING

A READ FOR GIST Read Yassir's email. Where is he and who is he talking about?

RE: How're things?
Sent: Friday November 10, 2017, 2:19 pm
To: a.nadar@screen.nett
From: YassirAwad@logbox.com

Hi Ahmed,

I'm having a great time at college! [a]___ There are about 20 people in my class, and all of them are friendly. There's a guy in my class named Erdem – he's from Turkey. He has long hair, a beard and he's really noisy, but he's very funny! He's one of my close friends now. [b]___ I met a French guy named Nico at soccer practice. He's really friendly, but very different from Erdem. He's fairly quiet and serious.

[c]___ The bad news is about my roommate. [d]___ His name's Erik. He's quiet in the day and noisy in the middle of the night! He's so unfriendly – he never speaks to me. And he's really messy! [e]___ I want to live with a happy, friendly and neat person!

See you soon,
Yassir

B READ FOR ORGANIZATION Read again. Match the sentences (1–5) with the blanks in the email (a–e). Use the information in the box to help you.

Reading for organization

To help you understand how a text is organized, think about how one sentence connects to another. Does it add more information? Does it explain something? Does it change topic?

1 I only have one roommate.
2 There's a lot of work to do, but there are also a lot of fun things to do in my free time.
3 I want to find a new place to live.
4 That's the good news.
5 I always laugh a lot when I'm with Erdem.

SPEAKING HUB

A Imagine you can choose a new roommate for Yassir. Think about the type of person Yassir wants to live with.

B PLAN Read about these people. Write notes about who would be a good/bad roommate for Yassir.

Antonio
Italian
'I'm from Naples, and I love cooking and soccer. I like listening to music when I study. I have lots of friends and I like to cook for them.'

Cvetomir
Bulgarian
'I love watching soccer on TV, but I never play. I never cook at home because I hate cleaning the kitchen. I like to sleep a lot. I'm a good roommate – I'm very quiet.'

Jonas
Swedish
'I like to study a lot in the day and talk to friends in the evening. My friends say I'm really funny, but I think I can be serious, too. I like to play sports and relax with friends on the weekend.'

C SPEAK Work in groups. Discuss the different people. Who is the best roommate for Yassir?

Describe family members and friends

2.4 Café chaos

F– make and respond to requests   P– stress and intonation

COMPREHENSION

A Look at the pictures. Then watch the video and check (✓) the things you see.

a camera ☐

keys ☐

a croissant ☐

a laptop ☐

headphones ☐

an umbrella ☐

a skateboard ☐

a phone ☐

B Work in pairs. Correct the wrong information in each sentence. Then watch the video again and check.

1 It's the ~~afternoon~~. *It's the morning.*
2 Gaby's cappuccino and croissant is £6.50.
3 Gaby has a skateboard.
4 Zac is from Detroit.
5 Gaby is Italian.
6 Gaby's mum's name is Maria.
7 Gaby has a flat.
8 Zac has a flat.

FUNCTIONAL LANGUAGE

Making and responding to requests

2.8 **A** Complete the phrases in the table with the words in the box. Then listen and check.

afraid ahead cappuccino dollars sit that

Asking for things
Can/Could I have a [1] ____________, please?
Can/Could I [2] ____________ here?
Saying Yes/No
Sure, no problem.
Go [3] ____________.
Of course.
No, sorry. I'm [4] ____________ not.
Asking for prices
How much is [5] ____________?
How much are they?
Giving prices
£4.50 / four pounds, fifty.
$2.20 / two [6] ____________ and twenty cents.
€15.75 / fifteen euros, seventy-five.

Glossary

mum **(n) (British)** = mom **(n) (American)**
pounds = **(British)** currency

B Work in pairs. Think of other ways of completing requests 1 and 2 in Exercise A. Practice saying them to each other.

Can I have a pen, please?

2.9 **C** How do you say the prices in the box? Practice with a partner, then listen and check.

£5.25 $6.50 €13.30 $8.90 £14.40 €17.70

D Work in pairs. Write down three different prices and say them to your partner. Write what you hear.

MILLY

SAM

NEENA

ZAC

GABY

USEFUL PHRASES

A Complete the useful phrases with the words in the box.

funny idea sorry this way wrong

a I am so ______________.

b No ______________!

c That's ______________!

d What's ______________?

e I have a great ______________.

f Let's do ______________!

B ▶ 00.58–05:17 Watch the second part of the video again and check your ideas in Exercise A.

PRONUNCIATION

Stress and intonation

A ▶ 00:00–00:58 Watch the first part of the video again and read the conversation. Notice the stress and intonation.

Sam: Morning. What can I get you?
Gaby: Hi! Can I have a cappuccino please?
Sam: Sure. Anything to eat?
Gaby: Could I have a brownie?
Sam: No, sorry. I'm afraid not. There aren't any.
Gaby: OK. Erm. Can I have a croissant then?
Sam: No problem. Is that everything?
Gaby: Yes, thanks. How much is that?
Sam: Four pounds fifty. Take a seat.
Gaby: Thank you.

B ▶ 00:00–00:58 Work in pairs. Watch again and repeat the conversation. Copy the stress and intonation.

C **SPEAK** Work in pairs. Practice the conversation in Exercise A. Remember to use the correct stress and intonation.

SPEAKING

A **PREPARE** Work in groups of three. Write your own café conversation.

- Student A is the café owner. Students B and C are customers.
- Use the phrases in Functional Language to help you.
- Include all of the words in the box below.

afraid ahead sit can you could I
course here can we sorry sure

B **DISCUSS** Practice your conversation. Perform it for the rest of the class.

A: Hello! Can I help you?
B: Hi! Can I have a coffee, please?
A: Sure, no problem.
B: And could I have a croissant?

Make and respond to requests

➤ Turn to page XXV to learn how to write an email to a friend.

Unit 2 Review

VOCABULARY

A Look at the family tree. Match the beginnings of sentences (1–8) with the ends of sentences (a–h).

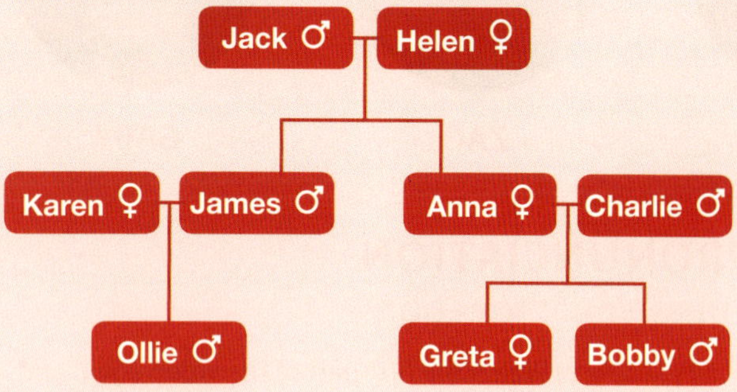

1	Anna is Greta's	a	granddaughter.
2	Greta is Bobby's	b	uncle.
3	Jack is Greta's	c	mother.
4	Helen is Jack's	d	grandfather.
5	Anna is Ollie's	e	cousin.
6	Greta is Helen's	f	wife.
7	Bobby is Ollie's	g	sister.
8	James is Bobby's	h	aunt.

B SPEAK Work in pairs. Tell your partner about your family.

C Complete the descriptions (1–4) with the words in the box.

beard curly light fat glasses long tall

1 Paolo has ______________, straight hair, blue eyes and a big ______________.
2 Julia has ______________ skin, brown eyes and blond, ______________ hair.
3 My grandfather is very ______________. He has gray hair and wears ______________.
4 My baby brother is very ______________.

D Complete sentences (1–6) with the words in the box.

funny messy noisy quiet serious neat

1 Laurence is so ______________! Why does she shout so much?
2 My brother is so ______________. His bedroom is full of dirty clothes and old pizza boxes.
3 Michael is really ______________. He always makes me laugh.
4 Your sister never smiles. Why is she so ______________ all the time?
5 Erin cleans the kitchen every day. She's a very ______________ person.
6 Why is he so ______________? I can't hear anything he says!

E Work in pairs. Describe:

- your best friend
- your teacher
- someone you work or study with

GRAMMAR

A Complete the text with pronouns or possessive adjectives.

Hi! [1] ______________'m Carrie. I'm Australian and I'm a doctor. [2] ______________ parents are Mike and Jennifer. [3] ______________'re actors. I have one sister. [4] ______________ name is Lula and [5] ______________'s 18. I have two brothers. [6] ______________ names are Tom and Brad. [7] ______________'re all from Brisbane.

B Correct the sentences by adding *'s* or *s'*.

1 Carrie*'s* last name is Pinto.
2 Her sister name is Lula.
3 Her brother names are Tom and Brad.
4 Jennifer children names are Carrie, Lula, Tom and Brad.
5 My brother dog is named Rufus.
6 His parent house is amazing!

C Complete the text with the correct form of *have/has*.

How many brothers and sisters [1] ______________ you [2] ______________? My family is small. It's just me, my brother, Eric and my mom. I look like my mom. She [3] ______________ blond hair and blue eyes. Eric [4] ______________ dark, curly hair, but I [5] ______________ blond, straight hair. My eyes are blue, like Mom's, but Eric [6] ______________ brown eyes.

D Find and correct one mistake in each sentence.

1 This is a ~~house~~ very big *house*.
2 My sisters are smalls.
3 I'm very quiet not.
4 He's a unfriendly really person.
5 Are you messy very?
6 Erin's quiet fairly today.

FUNCTIONAL LANGUAGE

A Reorder the words to make requests and offers.

1 I / please / have / a / Could / sandwich, / ?
Could I have a sandwich, please?
2 I / open / window / the / Can / ?
____
3 use / Can / please / I / dictionary, / your / ?
____
4 help / Would / me / you / like / to / ?
____

B Work in pairs. Take turns reading the situations and decide what to say. Make requests and offers.

1 Your friend has a very big bag.
2 You are cold.
3 You don't have a pen.
4 You are thirsty.

3 DAYS

> Yesterday's history, tomorrow's a mystery but today is a gift. That's why it's called the present.
>
> Alice Morse Earle

People walking through the snow in Tokyo, Japan.

OBJECTIVES

- talk about daily routines
- discuss daily activities
- describe a special day
- make and respond to suggestions
- write a blog post about your day

Work with a partner. Discuss the questions.

1 What's your favorite day of the year?
2 Look at the picture. Where is it?
3 What do you do on the weekend?

3.1 A typical day

● Talk about daily routines

V everyday activities **G** simple present positive **P** third person *-s*

LISTENING

A Read the information about a guest on the radio show *Two minutes*. Are the sentences true (T) or false (F)? Correct the false sentences.

1 Venus Mack works for a radio station. *T / F*
2 She's in her mid-thirties. *T / F*
3 She starts and finishes work in the afternoon. *T / F*
4 She's American. *T / F*

3.1 **B LISTEN FOR KEY WORDS** Listen to the radio show *Two minutes*. Match the names (1–3) with the nouns (a–c).

1 Bowie	a Venus's producer
2 Reuben	b Venus's dog
3 Joel	c a rock band

3.1 **C LISTEN FOR DETAIL** Listen to the interview again. Choose the correct time to complete the sentences.

1 I have breakfast at *4 pm / 6 pm*.
2 I get to work at *8 pm / 9 pm*.
3 The show starts at *10 am / 10 pm*.
4 I have coffee with friends at *6 am / 9 am*.
5 I go to bed at *2 am / 9 am*.

D SPEAK Work in pairs. Do you agree or disagree with these sentences? Why?

1 Venus's typical day is interesting.
2 Venus works long hours.
3 Venus has a lot of energy.

A: I agree. I think Venus's typical day is very exciting.
B: Why?
A: She meets a lot of musicians.

VOCABULARY

Everyday activities

A Look at the pictures of Tom's morning routine. Complete the phrases with the verbs in the box.

get get up ~~have~~ leave work

1 

I ______ at 7:00 am.

2 

I *have* breakfast at 7.30 am.

3 

I ______ home at 7:45 am.

4 

I ______ to work at 8:30 am.

5 

I ______ at a desk all day.

B Go to the **Vocabulary Hub** on **page XIX**.

C SPEAK Work in pairs. Take turns asking and answering questions with *What time do you ...?* and an everyday activity.

A: What time do you get up?
B: Seven o'clock.
A: What time do you have breakfast?
B: Seven thirty.

GRAMMAR

Simple present positive

A WORK IT OUT Read the sentences from *Two minutes*. Underline the verbs. Then cross out the incorrect rule in the box.

I get up at four o'clock.

Bowie comes with me.

I go to work by car.

My show starts at 10 pm.

Simple present

1 We use the simple present to talk about everyday habits and routines.
2 We use *be* + the main verb to make the simple present.
3 We add an *-s* (or *-es*) to verbs when the subject is *he, she* or *it*.

B Complete the table with the correct form of the verb *live*.

Simple present		
I/You/We/They	1 ______	in a small house.
He/She/It	2 ______	

C Go to the **Grammar Hub** on **page X**.

D SPEAK Work in pairs. Think about someone you know. Tell your partner about their typical day.

A: My sister gets up at six o'clock.

B: My friend Lukas plays video games every night.

PRONUNCIATION

third person -s

3.2 **A** There are three different ways of pronouncing the endings of simple present verbs in the third person. Can you hear the difference? Listen and repeat.

1 /s/ She **works** in an office.
2 /z/ He **plays** video games every night.
3 /ɪz/ He **watches** the news every morning.

3.3 **B** Listen to the sentences. Circle the correct pronunciation of the third person *-s* ending.

1	She **leaves** home at 8 am.	/s/ /z/ /ɪz/
2	He **teaches** French at the university.	/s/ /z/ /ɪz/
3	She **gets** home at seven o'clock.	/s/ /z/ /ɪz/
4	He **goes** to bed late on the weekend.	/s/ /z/ /ɪz/
5	She **washes** her hair twice a week.	/s/ /z/ /ɪz/
6	He **looks** like Johnny Depp!	/s/ /z/ /ɪz/

3.3 **C** Listen again and repeat the sentences. Be careful to pronounce the third person *-s* endings correctly.

SPEAKING

A PREPARE Work in pairs. Make a list of five interesting or exciting jobs.

B PLAN Choose one of the jobs in Exercise A. Write sentences to explain a typical day for someone with that job.

- She gets up at six in the morning.
- She goes to the studio at eight o'clock.
- She talks to the actors.

C SPEAK Work in new pairs. Read your sentences and try to guess the job.

A: She gets up at six o'clock in the morning. She goes to the studio at eight o'clock. She talks to the actors …

B: She's a movie director!

A: Correct!

Talk about daily routines

3.2 All day, every day

Discuss daily activities

G adverbs of frequency   P word stress   V prepositions of time

READING

A Work in pairs. Look at the photos. Which of the activities do you do every day?

B **READ FOR MAIN IDEA** Read *Lifestyle online*. Choose the correct option to complete the definition of *essential*.

> **essential** (adj.) = something you *learn / need*

C Read the comments on *Lifestyle online*. What four daily essentials do they write about that are not in the *Top 10 daily essentials* list?

D **READ FOR DETAIL** Read the comments again. Are the sentences true (T) or false (F)? Correct the false sentences.

1 Milos thinks breakfast is essential. *T / F*
2 Scotgirl eats breakfast every day. *T / F*
3 Topdog44 isn't a soccer fan. *T / F*
4 Lisab needs to exercise every day. *T / F*
5 Celine drinks black coffee every night. *T / F*

E **SPEAK** Work with a partner. Make a list of your top ten daily essentials.

GRAMMAR

Adverbs of frequency

A Complete the sentences with adverbs from the text.

1 I ________________ eat breakfast, but not every day.
2 I ________________ watch soccer on TV.
3 I'm ________________ away from my friends and family.
4 I ________________ exercise, @Lisab!

B **WORK IT OUT** Read the sentences in Exercise A and complete the rules.

> **Adverbs of frequency**
>
> 1 We put adverbs of frequency ***before / after*** main verbs.
> 2 We put adverbs of frequency ***before / after*** the verb *be*.

Lifestyle *online*

What do you use every day? What couldn't you live without? We asked 100 people for their top 10 daily essentials. Here's what they said …

Top 10 daily essentials

1	the internet	6	a cell phone
2	a shower or bath	7	a good friend
3	TV	8	a cup of coffee or tea
4	laptop or tablet	9	breakfast
5	a car	10	a pet

Milos
For me, I need a good breakfast and soccer on TV.

Scotgirl
LOL @Milos! I sometimes eat breakfast, but not every day. For me, it's music. I always listen to music on my way to work.

Topdog44
I never watch soccer on TV. I think it's really boring. I need my cell phone. It's an essential – no question.

Fumi
For me, Facebook is essential. I travel a lot for work, so I'm often away from my friends and family. I use Facebook to talk to friends and send pictures of the places I travel to.

Lisab
Hmm … interesting question! For me, it's exercise. I usually do yoga for an hour before work.

Celine
Haha! I rarely exercise, @Lisab! Coffee is my daily essential. I always start my day with a cup of strong, black coffee. I couldn't live without it.

C Go to the **Grammar Hub** on **page X**.

D **SPEAK** Work in pairs. Write five sentences about yourself using adverbs of frequency. Tell your partner.

A: I rarely watch TV.
B: Really? I watch TV every day.

LISTENING

A PREDICT What is a 'screen-free week'? Discuss your ideas with a partner. Then read the search result and check.

What's going on?

Screen-free week

November 7, 2017 Most people these days spend at least 15 hours every week online or on their phones. Well, May 2–8, join us and other people around the world in screen-free week – a week when people take a break from screens and the internet. No cell phone, no internet and no TV. There is life beyond the screen!

3.4 **B LISTEN FOR GIST** Listen to a conversation between Ali and Ian. Does Ali want to do screen-free week? Why/Why not?

3.4 **C LISTEN FOR DETAIL** Listen again. Are the sentences true (T) or false (F)? Correct the false sentences.

1. Ali spends nine hours a week on his phone. T / F
2. He looks at his phone when he wakes up. T / F
3. He uses his phone at work. T / F
4. He plays games online with his friends. T / F
5. He never watches soccer on TV. T / F

D SPEAK Work in pairs. Answer the questions.

1. How often do you check your phone?
2. Do you think you need a screen-free week? Why/Why not?

PRONUNCIATION

Word stress

3.5 **A** Listen and repeat. Stress the underlined syllables.

●•	•●	●••	•●•
morning	online	internet	computer
open	begin	Saturday	umbrella

3.6 **B** Add the words in the box to the table in Exercise A. Then listen and check your answers.

before chocolate essential grandmother laptop rarely relax routine serious unfriendly usually

3.6 **C** Listen again and repeat the words.

VOCABULARY

Prepositions of time

A Look at the phrases from the conversation between Ali and Ian. Then complete the rules with the correct preposition, *in*, *on* or *at*.

1. *... from early* **in** *the morning to late* **at** *night.*
2. **On** *Saturday and Sunday, it's non-stop soccer!*
3. **On** *the weekend, we watch soccer on TV.*

Prepositions of time

1. We use ________ with a time period (the morning, the afternoon, the summer, 1990, etc).
2. We use ________ with the day of the week (Monday, Tuesday, etc) and dates.
3. We use ________ with exact times (6 pm, noon, etc).

B Write the correct preposition of time next to the words.

1. ________ Sunday
2. ________ three o'clock
3. ________ March 6
4. ________ the evening
5. ________ June
6. ________ my birthday

SPEAKING

A PLAN Work in pairs. Think of ten activities to do during screen-free week.

B PREPARE Make a top ten list. Put the most essential activity at number 1.

C Work in pairs. Discuss your lists from Exercise A. Agree on the top five essentials.

A: I think 'go for a run' is the most essential. I need to do lots of exercise.
B: Really? I'm not sure. What about 'spend time with friends' as number one?

Discuss daily activities

3.3 A special day

Describe a special day

G simple present negative **P** sentence stress **V** big celebrations **S** listening for detail

READING

A Work in pairs. Look at the pictures in *A birthday to remember* and answer the questions.

1 What can you see in the pictures?
2 Which country are these things from?

B SCAN Read *A birthday to remember* quickly to check your answers to Exercise A.

C READ FOR GIST Read *A birthday to remember* again and answer the questions.

1 Why is Katie in China?
2 Which festival does she write about?
3 Is she enjoying her birthday?

D READ FOR DETAIL Read *A birthday to remember* again. Find and correct five more mistakes in the summary.

> Katie sometimes celebrates her birthday with ~~friends~~ *her mom*. This year, she is on vacation in China, and it is the time of the Moon Festival. The festival happens on the same day every September, and it is 150 years old. People wear traditional clothes. They eat mooncakes and watch dancers in modern costumes. They light lanterns to say thank you to their grandparents. Katie loves Moon Festival. She thinks this a good birthday.

Compass Travel

A birthday to remember

July 7 | Leave a comment

I don't usually celebrate my birthday. I sometimes go out for a birthday lunch with my mom, but I usually just take it easy. My best friend doesn't understand, but for me, my birthday is no big deal. But this year, my birthday is a little different. I'm on vacation in China at the moment, and my birthday is on the same day as the Moon Festival. It's really cool.

Moon Festival is also called Mid-Autumn Festival, and people in China celebrate it every September or October. It's on a different day every year, but there's always a full moon. The festival is more than 3,000 years old. It's amazing, and really colorful – I love it! The people don't wear traditional clothes, but they eat traditional food, like mooncakes. They are small, round cakes and they're delicious! You can see dancers in colorful costumes perform traditional dances. There are also lots of paper lanterns with bright patterns. People light them to say thank you for children, who make everyone so happy – most of the time! So far, this birthday is one of the best ever!

1 ______________

2 ______________

GRAMMAR

Simple present negative

A WORK IT OUT Look at the sentences from *A birthday to remember* and complete the table with *don't* or *doesn't*.

*I **don't** usually celebrate my birthday.*
*My best friend **doesn't** understand, …*
*The people **don't** wear traditional clothes, …*

Simple present negative		
I/You/We/They	1 ______________	eat special food.
He/She/It	2 ______________	

B Go to the **Grammar Hub** on **page X**.

C SPEAK Work in pairs. Write three negative simple present sentences – two true, one false. Then read them to your partner. Guess which sentence is false.

A: I don't speak French. I don't watch TV. I don't eat meat.
B: The second one is false. You always watch TV!

PRONUNCIATION

Sentence stress

3.7 **A** Listen and repeat. Then underline the stressed words.

1 I like festivals. 2 I don't like festivals.

B Look at the underlined words in Exercise A. Complete the rules.

Sentence stress in simple present

1 In short simple present positive sentences, we usually stress the *main verb / noun*.
2 In short simple present negative sentences, we usually stress the *auxiliary verb (don't/doesn't) / main verb*.

3 ______________

6 ______________

7 ______________

4 ______________

5 ______________

C Read the conversations. Underline the stressed words. Then listen and check. (3.8)

1 Katia: Do you like mooncakes?
Bian: Yes, but I don't eat them often.

2 Amelia: Do you like New Year's Eve?
Lizzie: Uh, yes. I like the fireworks.

D SPEAK Work in pairs. Practice the conversations in Exercise C. Be careful to stress the words correctly.

VOCABULARY
Big celebrations

A Match the pictures (1–7) with the words in the box.

decorations fireworks parade party present special food traditional clothes

B Complete the questions with the words in the box.

eat give have put up wear

1 Do you usually ______________ a party on your birthday?
2 When do you ______________ decorations?
3 Do you ______________ special food on New Year's Day?
4 When do people ______________ traditional clothes in your country?
5 When do you ______________ presents in your country?

C SPEAK Work in pairs. Answer the questions in Exercise B.

LISTENING

A LISTEN FOR KEY WORDS Listen to a conversation about big celebrations. Which words from Vocabulary Exercise A do they talk about? (3.9)

B LISTEN FOR DETAIL Listen to the conversation again and choose the correct options to complete the sentences. Use the information in the box to help you. (3.9)

> **Listening for detail**
>
> Sometimes we need to listen for specific information (e.g. what time something opens, etc). Use these ideas to help you listen for detail:
> - Read the questions carefully.
> - Underline key words.
> - Listen carefully for the key words that you underlined.

1 Mexico celebrates Independence Day in *September* / *December*.
2 All of the stores and banks *open* / *close* for the party.
3 In the evening, people go to watch *a big parade* / *the fireworks*.
4 At home, people put up red, white and *green* / *blue* decorations.
5 Carlos *wears* / *doesn't wear* traditional clothes to dance in.

SPEAKING HUB

A PREPARE Think of a special day. It could be:
- a birthday
- a religious day
- a national holiday
- a festival

B PLAN Write notes. Think about:
- the food you eat
- the music you listen to
- the clothes you wear
- the presents you give
- the songs you sing
- the people you see

C DISCUSS Work in groups. Describe your day. Compare your festivals.

In Japan, families often eat KFC together on Christmas!

Really? We eat together, but we don't eat fried chicken!

Describe a special day

3.4 Finding Neena

F– make and respond to suggestions P– stress and intonation

COMPREHENSION

A ▶ Watch the video and answer the questions.

1 Who lives in the flat? ____________
2 Who wants to live in the flat? ____________
3 When do they agree to move in? ____________
4 How many bathrooms are there? ____________
5 What time does Zac start work? ____________
6 What time does Neena get up? ____________

B Look at the pictures. Which flat (a–c) is the one in the video?

C ▶ 00:29–01:30 Work in pairs. Complete the advertisement. Then watch part of the video again and check your answers.

D ▶ 02:40–03:25 Put Zac's morning routine in the correct order (1–7). Then watch part of the video again and check your answers.

__ have a shower
__ start work
__ wake up
__ have a coffee
__ finish work
__ brush teeth
__ have breakfast

E SPEAK Work in pairs. Compare your morning routine to Zac's.

A: I wake up at 8 am, not 9. What about you?
B: I wake up at 6 am! When do you start work?

FUNCTIONAL LANGUAGE

Making and responding to suggestions

Complete the phrases with the words in the box. There are two words you do not need.

about don't getting up let's moving in not sounds sure

Make suggestions	Say *yes*
What/How [1] ________ this apartment?	[5] ________ good/great.
What/How about [2] ________ next week?	Looks good/great!
Why [3] ________ we email her/go now?	Great!
[4] ________ call her.	Awesome!
	Say *no*
	I'm not [6] ________.

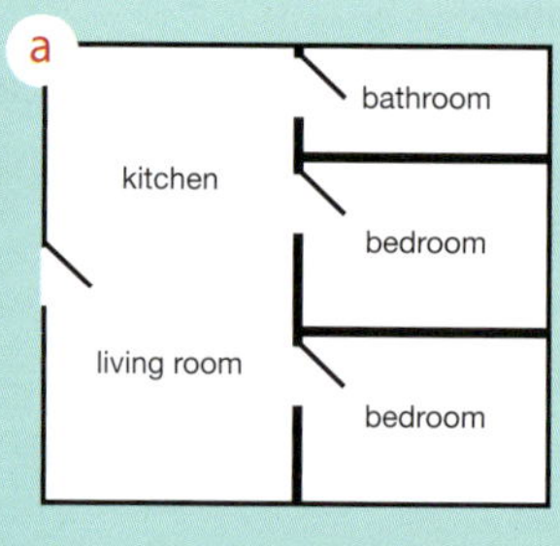

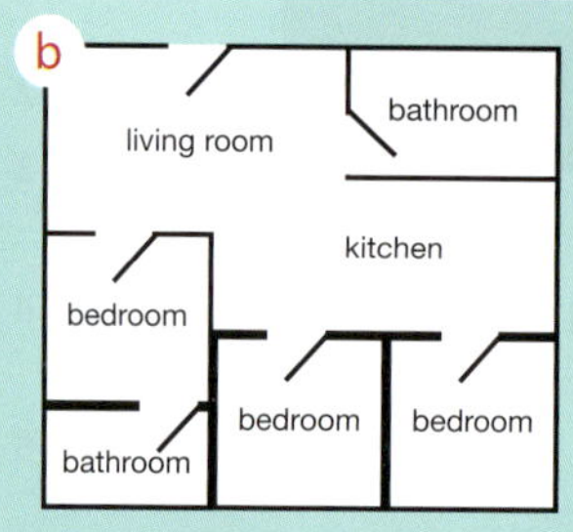

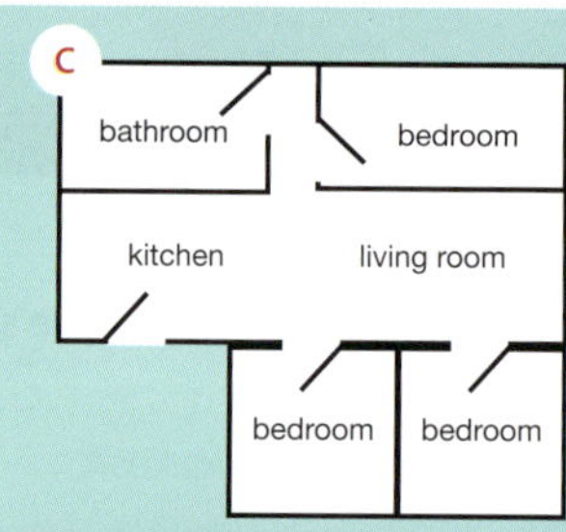

Beautiful flat | £190 pw
Single room(s) | Clapham Common (SW4)

Please call
0770 090 [9] ________.

Hi. I'm [1] ________. I need [2] ________ lovely new housemates. I live in a [3] ________ bedroom flat on Park [4] ________. I'm [5] ________. I like [6] ________, [7] ________ and playing [8] ________ games.

Glossary

housemates **(n) (British)** = roommates **(n) (American)**
lovely **(adj) (British)** = nice **(adj) (American)**
flat **(n) (British)** = apartment **(n) (American)**
have a shower **(British)** = take a shower **(American)**

MILLY

SAM

NEENA

ZAC

GABY

USEFUL PHRASES

Choose the correct definition of each useful phrase.

1 Any luck?
 a Are you lucky? b Were you successful?
2 Cool!
 a Great! b It's cold!
3 Of course.
 a Yes. b No.
4 Actually, …
 a At the moment, b In fact, …
5 It's not far.
 a It's near here. b It isn't near here.
6 Lucky you!
 a I want to do that! b I don't want to do that!

PRONUNCIATION

Stress and intonation

A 00:00–02:20 Watch the first part of the video again. Complete the conversations (A–C).

A
Gaby: Hey, [1]________ this [2]________? It's nice.
Zac: Hmmm … [3]________ sure. It's very small.

B
Gaby: [4]________ good. [5]________ email [6]________?
Zac: No, [7]________ call [8]________!

C
Zac: Can we see the apartment today?
Neena: Of course. Actually, it's not far. [9]________ now?
Zac: [10]________ great!
Gaby: Brilliant! Let's go!

B 00:00–02:20 Watch again and repeat the conversations. Copy the stress and intonation.

C **SPEAK** Work in pairs. Practice the conversations in Exercise A. Remember to use the correct stress and intonation.

SPEAKING

A **PREPARE** Work in pairs. Complete the suggestions for what to do after school. Use the ideas in parentheses.

- What about going to ________ (*a place*)?
- Let's eat ________ (*food*).
- Why don't we watch ________ (*a movie*)?
- How about listening to ________ (*a band / music*)?
- Let's play ________ (*a game*).

B **DISCUSS** Go around the class and make suggestions to your classmates. Reply using the Functional language phrases.

A: How about going to a concert?
B: Awesome!

Make and respond to suggestions

➤ Turn to page XXVI to learn how to write a blog post about your day.

Unit 3 Review

VOCABULARY

A Complete the sentences with the words in the box.

get to   get up   have   leave   work

1 I _______________ in a large office in King's Cross.
2 I usually _______________ toast and coffee for breakfast.
3 I _______________ at 6:30 every morning.
4 I try to _______________ home before seven o'clock.
5 I _______________ work between nine and nine thirty.

B Match the verbs (1–8) with the words (a–h) to make phrases describing everyday activities.

1 have	a to music / to the radio
2 get	b in a house / in an apartment
3 listen	c a book / a magazine
4 watch	d to work / to bed / for a run
5 live	e up early / home from work
6 read	f for a bank / in Spain
7 work	g breakfast / lunch
8 go	h a movie / TV

C Complete the sentences with the correct prepositions.

1 I usually watch the news ______ the afternoon.
2 I sometimes listen to music ______ night.
3 I sometimes go for a walk ______ the weekend.
4 I have an English class ______ Tuesday.
5 I read the newspaper ______ the morning.
6 I rarely work ______ Fridays.

D Complete the sentences with the words in the box.

decorations   fireworks   parade   party
presents   special food   traditional clothes

1 What are you doing on Saturday? Do you want to come to a _______________?
2 It's sad, but many people don't wear _______________ at the festival anymore.
3 My mom spends three days cooking so we can have _______________ on the big day.
4 My family doesn't put up _______________ until December 24th.
5 We usually open all of the _______________ after breakfast.
6 There's a big _______________ through the streets with giant balloons, dancers and people wearing costumes.
7 We don't have _______________ on New Year's Eve anymore because they scare the dog.

GRAMMAR

A Complete the paragraph with the correct form of the verbs in the box.

get (x2)   go (x3)   have   leave   live   work (x2)   take

Luke Timms [1]__________ six days a week and his days are usually the same. He [2]__________ in a small apartment in Milan. He [3]__________ up early every day and [4]__________ a shower. He [5]__________ breakfast and then [6]__________ the apartment at around eight. He [7]__________ to work by motorcycle. He [8]__________ for a television station in the city center. He finishes work at 6:30 pm. He [9]__________ home around 7 pm and [10]__________ for a long run. He usually [11]__________ to bed at around midnight.

B Rewrite the sentences with the adverbs in parentheses.

1 I get up at 6 am. (usually)
_____ *I usually get up at 6 am.* _____
2 I go for a walk in the park. (often)
____
3 I watch TV. (sometimes)
____
4 I am late for my English class. (never)
____
5 I have breakfast at 7 am. (always)
____
6 I am late for work. (rarely)
____

C Rewrite the sentences to make them negative.

1 We go to work.
_____ *We don't go to work.* _____
2 People eat special food.
____
3 We dance.
____
4 People wear special clothes.
____
5 People stay at home.
____

FUNCTIONAL LANGUAGE

Complete the phrases with the words in the box.

~~about~~   how   idea   let's   sounds   why

1 What ____ *about* ____ going out for a meal?
2 _______________ good, but I'm not hungry.
3 _______________ about watching a movie?
4 _______________ don't we stay in?
5 That's a great _______________!
6 _______________ have a nice cup of tea!

4 WORK AND EDUCATION

> Choose a job you love and you'll never have to work a day in your life.
>
> Confucius

Firefighters at work in London, UK.

OBJECTIVES

- talk about jobs
- talk about the perfect job
- talk about adult education and career development
- ask for someone and leave a message
- write an email asking for information

Work with a partner. Discuss the questions.

1 Do you like your job?

2 Look at the picture. Do you think this is an easy job? Why/Why not?

3 Would you like to do this job?

4.1 What do you do?

Talk about jobs

V work and jobs **G** simple present *yes/no* questions; short answers **P** linking sounds: *do/does*

VOCABULARY
Work and jobs

A Match the pictures (1–4) with the words in the box.

doctor engineer pilot teacher

B Go to the **Vocabulary Hub** on **page XIX**.

C Complete the sentences with the words in the box.

computer home meet meetings office travel (x2) wear (x2)

1 I sometimes ______________ for my job, but I usually work in an ______________. I go to ______________ and I meet a lot of different people.
2 I like my job because I ______________ new people every day. I ______________ a uniform. I don't work in an office – I work in a hospital.
3 I always ______________ for my job, but I usually work with the same people. I ______________ a uniform and I go to a lot of different places.
4 I usually work from ______________. I sometimes go out to meet people. I spend a lot of time on my ______________.

D SPEAK Work in pairs. Talk about your job or the job of someone you know. Use the words and phrases in Exercise C to help you.

A: I'm a designer. I don't work in an office. I work from home.
B: My sister is a businessperson. She travels a lot for her work. She always goes to different places.

READING

A READ FOR GIST Read the interview. Are the sentences true (T) or false (F)? Correct the false sentences.

1 He's a nurse. *T / F*
2 He works in an office. *T / F*
3 He sometimes works from home. *T / F*
4 He loves his job. *T / F*

B READ FOR DETAIL Read the interview again. Find and correct mistakes in the summary.

Matheus is an engineer. He works in an office, but he also goes to meetings and he visits hospitals. He doesn't work from home because he never needs to talk to other people. He works for a small company in the US. He never visits other countries. He says his job is easy, but he loves it because it's unusual.

C SPEAK Talk to your partner. Do you think Matheus has an interesting job? Why/Why not?

Working Week – Out for lunch

Every week, we catch someone on their lunch break and ask them five quick questions about their job.

This week: Matheus Oliveira, 32

What's your job?
I'm an engineer, like my brother.

Does your brother work for the same company as you?
No, he doesn't. He works for a big company in the US.

Do you work in an office?
Yes, I do. I also spend a lot of time out of the office. I go to meetings and I visit factories.

Do you work from home sometimes?
No, I don't. I always need to talk to other people, so I don't stay at home.

Do you travel for work?
Yes, sometimes. I work for a large company in Brazil, but I often go to the US, China and Japan.

Do you like your job?
Yes, I love it. It's difficult, but it's also interesting and exciting. I'm very lucky.

GRAMMAR

Simple present *yes/no* questions; short answers

A Work in pairs. Look at the questions and short answers from the interview. Underline the main verbs in the questions. What is at the beginning of each question?

1 Do you work in an office? Yes, I do.
2 Do you work from home sometimes? No, I don't.
3 Do you travel for work? Yes, sometimes.
4 Does your brother work for the same company as you? No, he doesn't.

B Complete the rules with the words in the box.

do/does (x2)   *don't/doesn't*   the main verb

Simple present – *yes/no* questions; short answers

- To form questions in the simple present, we use [1] __________ + subject + [2] __________.
- In affirmative short answers, we use [3] __________.
- In negative short answers, we use [4] __________.

C Correct the mistakes in the questions and answers.

1	A: Do you go to meetings?	B: Yes, do I.
2	A: Do they work in the same office?	B: Yes, they don't.
3	A: Does you work from home?	B: Yes, sometimes.
4	A: Do she have lunch in a café?	B: Yes, she does.
5	A: Do you meet a lot of new people?	B: Yes, I meet.

D Use the prompts to write simple present questions.

1 you / work in an office?
Do you work in an office?
2 you / wear a uniform?
____
3 you / travel for your job?
____
4 you / work with people?
____
5 you / like your job?
____
6 anyone in your family / have an interesting job?
____

E Go to the **Grammar Hub** on **page XII**.

F **SPEAK** Ask and answer the questions in Exercise D. Use information about yourself, or imagine you are someone else.

A: Do you work in an office?
B: Yes, I do. It's in the city center.
A: Does anyone in your family have an interesting job?
B: Yes, my brother does! He's a police officer.

PRONUNCIATION

Linking sounds: *do/does*

4.1 **A** Listen to the questions and answers. Notice how some sounds link together.

/ʤʊ/	Do‿you like your job?	Yes, I do.
	Do‿you work from home?	No, I don't.
/dʌziː/	Does‿he travel for his job?	Yes, he does.
/dʌzʃiː/	Does‿she work long hours?	No, she doesn't.

4.2 **B** Listen to the questions again and repeat. Link the sounds together.

C **SPEAK** Complete the questions with your own ideas, and then ask and answer with a partner. Remember to link sounds together.

1 Do you …
2 Do you …
3 Does he …
4 Does she …

SPEAKING

A **PREPARE** Work in groups. Write ten *yes/no* questions that will help you guess someone's job.

1 Do you work in an office?
2 Do you wear a uniform?
3 Do you work with other people?

B **SPEAK** Follow the steps below to play the game.

Student 1: Choose a job. Don't tell the other students.

Other students: Ask Student 1 the questions. You must guess the job in ten questions (or fewer).

Student 1: Answer the questions. You can only say *Yes, I do.* or *No, I don't.*

A: Do you work outside?
B: No, I don't.
A: Do you work with people?
B: Yes, I do.

C **SPEAK** Change roles and repeat.

Talk about jobs

4.2 Good job!

Talk about the perfect job

G *have to / don't have to* **P** connected speech: *have to* **V** time expressions

Good job / Bad job

Everyone wants to have a good job, but what exactly does a 'good job' mean? Is it the money, the location or the hours? What about the company culture? We speak to two people with very different jobs to find out more.

Jie Chen

I work for a small company, and the office is near my house, so I don't have to take the subway or drive my car. I walk to work every day, and it only takes five minutes!

I really like the office. It's a nice space, and it's very quiet and relaxing. Also, there's an outside space, so we don't have to stay indoors on sunny days – we can work outside!

My salary isn't great, but it's okay. My favorite thing about my job is that I can choose my own hours. I don't have to work nine to five! I usually work from seven in the morning until three in the afternoon. I'm a morning person, so I'm very happy that I can work early, and get home early, too.

Glossary

nine to five (n phrase) the hours of a typical working day in many countries

salary (n) the fixed amount of money that you get for your job

self-employed (adj) working for yourself, not for one company

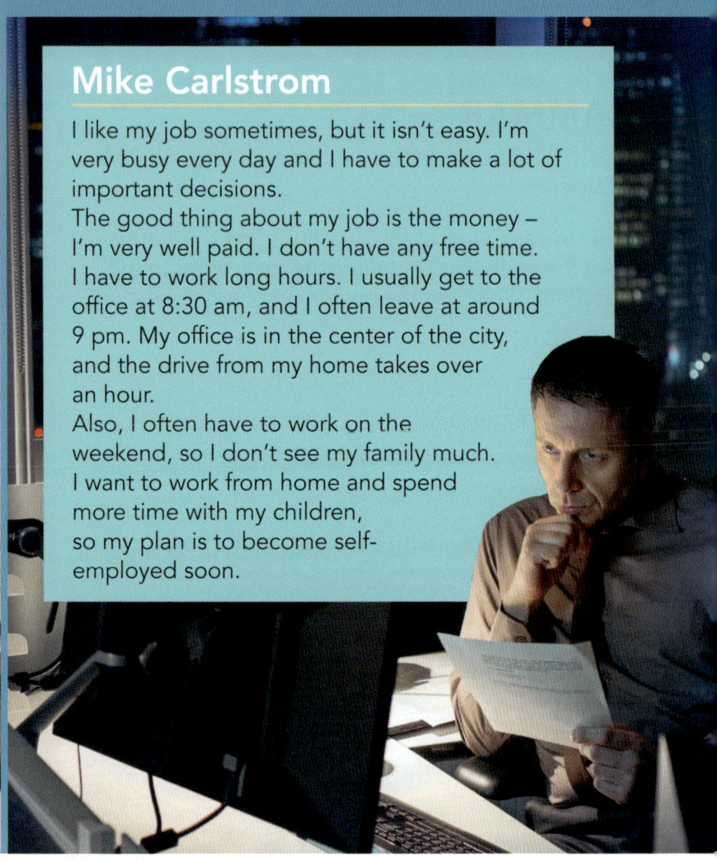

Mike Carlstrom

I like my job sometimes, but it isn't easy. I'm very busy every day and I have to make a lot of important decisions.

The good thing about my job is the money – I'm very well paid. I don't have any free time. I have to work long hours. I usually get to the office at 8:30 am, and I often leave at around 9 pm. My office is in the center of the city, and the drive from my home takes over an hour.

Also, I often have to work on the weekend, so I don't see my family much. I want to work from home and spend more time with my children, so my plan is to become self-employed soon.

READING

A Work in pairs. Rank the things in the box in order of importance for a job (1 = very important, 4 = not important).

___ colleagues/boss ___ money ___ hours ___ location

B READ FOR GIST Read an article about jobs. Which of the things in Exercise A do the two people talk about?

C READ FOR DETAIL Read the article again. Are the sentences true (T) or false (F)? Correct the false sentences.

1 Both Jie and Mike make a lot of money. *T / F*
2 Jie and Mike travel to work in different ways. *T / F*
3 Jie likes working in the evening. *T / F*
4 Jie and Mike work the same hours. *T / F*
5 Jie can work outside sometimes. *T / F*
6 Both Jie and Mike's jobs are quiet and relaxing. *T / F*

D SPEAK Work with a partner. Discuss Jie and Mike's jobs. Talk about:

- the good things about their jobs
- the bad things about their jobs

A: Mike has a good salary. *B: Yes, but the hours are long.*

GRAMMAR

have to / don't have to

A Complete the sentences with verbs from the article.

1 I don't have to ______________ the subway or ______________ my car.
2 I don't have to ______________ nine to five!
3 I have to ______________ a lot of important decisions.
4 I often have to ______________ on the weekend.

B Look at the sentences in Exercise A. Choose the correct option to complete the rule.

have to / don't have to

We use *have* or *has to* to talk about rules and things we ***need / don't need*** to do.

C Go to the **Grammar Hub** on **page XII**.

PRONUNCIATION

Connected speech: *have to*

4.3 **A** Listen to the questions. Is there a pause between 'have' and 'to'?

1 Do you have‿to work long hours?

2 Do employees have‿to eat in the company restaurant?

4.4 **B** Listen and repeat the questions.

1 Do you have to wear a uniform?

2 Does he have to go to a lot of meetings?

3 Do they have to organize a lot of trips?

4 Do you have to ask your boss for a vacation?

C SPEAK Write four questions using *have to*. Work with a partner and ask your questions.

A: Do you have to work on weekends?

B: No I don't! I only have to work nine to five, Monday to Friday.

LISTENING

4.5 **A LISTEN FOR GIST** Listen to the conversation between Hussam and Salah. Which picture is Hussam's work?

4.5 **B LISTEN FOR DETAIL** Listen again and complete each sentence with one word.

1 Hussan usually starts ______________ at noon.

2 He usually takes it easy in the ______________.

3 He sometimes has ______________ at 1pm.

4 He can decide when to ______________ work.

5 He is self-employed so he works from ______________.

C SPEAK Work with a partner. Do you want a job like Hussam's? Why/Why not?

VOCABULARY

Time expressions

A Read the sentences from the conversation. Match the time expressions in **bold** with the times (1–5).

*I don't have to work **nine to five**.*

*I usually start work at **noon.***

*I have to start really **early in the morning**.*

*I don't go to bed until **midnight** or later.*

*...other days, I eat **late in the afternoon**.*

1 12 pm *noon*

2 4 pm – 6 pm ______________

3 9 am – 5 pm ______________

4 12 am ______________

5 5 am – 9 am ______________

B Complete the sentences with the time expressions from Exercise A.

1 I work better at night. Sometimes I study late in the evenings, until ______________ or later.

2 I don't have to work from ______________, like my friends in offices. It's great!

3 I have lunch at ______________ every day. I start early in the morning, so I'm always hungry by then.

4 I find it difficult to think ______________. I just want to go home and relax.

5 I like to go for a run ______________ before I go to work.

C SPEAK Work with a partner. Write five questions using the words and phrases from Exercise A. Ask and answer the questions with your partner.

A: Do you have to work from nine to five?

B: No, I can choose my own hours.

SPEAKING

A PLAN Make a list of five things that make a good job.

1 A big salary!

2 The people you work with.

B SPEAK Work in small groups. Compare your ideas from Exercise A. Together, decide on a top five list.

C PRESENT Read your list to the class. Explain your ideas.

1

2

Talk about the perfect job

Talk about adult education and career development

G – question words P – word stress: questions V – education collocations S – listening for gist

The Open University

It's never too late to learn something new. The Open University is the largest university in the UK, with almost 174,000 students in 2015/2016 alone. It is a distance learning university, and it's for anyone who wants to study and learn a new skill.

FAQs

Who are the courses for?
Open University degree courses are open for anyone. Many people who have jobs or cannot go to a normal university on weekdays choose to study with us. As a distance learning university, it's perfect for anyone who wants to study from home.

How much does it cost?
The cost of full-time study is almost half that of other universities in the UK.

What subjects do you teach?
There are nearly 500 courses to choose from.

When do students go to classes?
Students don't 'go' to classes. All of the classes and resources are available online or through print and video sources, so students can access them when they need to.

Where do students meet their teachers?
They don't. Students usually send homework to their teachers. The teachers reply by email.

How long does an average degree course take?
It takes an average of six years for most students to finish their degrees.

Why do people take distance learning courses?
A lot of people work during the day and study in their free time. The Open University is flexible. You can study anywhere, anytime.

Glossary

course (n) a series of lessons in one subject
degree (n) a certification you get after you complete a university course
resources (n) things you can use to help you to study
skill (n) the ability to do something well
university (n) a place where adults study

READING

A Work with a partner. Discuss the questions.

1 Why do people with a job study in their free time?
2 What kinds of things do they study?

B READ FOR GIST Read the webpage about the Open University. How is it different from a typical university?

C READ FOR DETAIL Read the webpage again. Work in pairs. What do these numbers refer to?

1 174,000 2 500 3 6

D Read the webpage again. Are the sentences true (T) or false (F)? Correct the false sentences.

1 The Open University is the largest university in Europe. T / F
2 It's only for British people. T / F
3 You study when you want to. T / F
4 Students don't usually meet their teachers. T / F
5 A lot of people study during the day. T / F

GRAMMAR

Question words

A Look at the questions on the webpage. Complete the rules with the question words in the box.

How long How much What When Where Who ~~Why~~

Question words

1 __Why__ to ask for a reason.
2 ________ to ask a question about a thing.
3 ________ to ask a question about a place.
4 ________ to ask a question about a person.
5 ________ to ask a question about quantity.
6 ________ to ask about a length of time.
7 ________ to ask a question about a time.

B Go to the Grammar Hub on page XII.

C Complete the questions with words from Exercise A.

1 ________ subjects are popular in your country?
2 ________ are they so popular?
3 ________ can you get information about courses?
4 ________ does it cost to go to this university?
5 ________ do people usually start and finish classes?
6 ________ do people usually study for (e.g. three years, four years, etc)?
7 ________ is your favorite teacher? Why?

D SPEAK Ask and answer the questions in Exercise C.

PRONUNCIATION
Word stress: questions

4.6 Listen and repeat the questions. Underline the stressed words.

1 Where do you work?
2 Why do you study history?
3 When do you start work?
4 What do you do?
5 How much does your course cost?

LISTENING

4.7 **A LISTEN FOR GIST** Listen to a conversation. Choose the correct summary (1–3).

Listening for gist

Gist is the main idea. When you listen for gist, you don't need to understand every word. Listen for key words, which help you to understand the main idea(s) and summarize what you heard.

1 Lily is a teacher. She wants to teach art history to Tom.
2 Lily works in an office. She wants to teach art history like Tom.
3 Lily wants to study art history at a university so she can work in an office.

4.7 **B LISTEN FOR DETAIL** Listen again. Match the beginnings of sentences (1–5) with the ends of sentences (a–e).

1 I recommend online
2 We offer over
3 You send your homework to us
4 You study when
5 You pay for access to our online

a by email.
b materials.
c classes.
d 800 courses.
e you want.

C SPEAK Work in groups. Discuss the questions.

1 How long do you have to study to become a teacher in your country?
2 Who pays for it?

VOCABULARY
Education collocations

A Choose the correct verbs to complete the sentences.

1 I want to ***take / get*** a course in my free time.
2 I don't want to ***study / train*** a subject I don't like!
3 I want to ***train / do*** to be a teacher.
4 I want to ***go / study*** to a university.
5 I have to ***take / get*** a lot of exams.
6 Then, after two more years, I can ***study / get*** a degree.
7 My company says I have to ***take / get*** a certification.

B Underline the verb–noun collocations in Exercise A.

SPEAKING HUB

A PLAN Work in small groups. Imagine you are planning a new course for adults who want to retrain.

- Think about the types of jobs that adults retrain for in your country.
- Choose the type of course (for example, English, science, business).

B PREPARE Plan the course. Decide on your answers to these questions:

- When will the course happen? (weekdays, weekends, any time)
- Where? (in a college, at a university, online)
- How long will it take?
- How much will it cost?
- What exams do students have to take?
- What certifications do they get?

C DISCUSS Imagine you are at a career fair.

- Present your course to the rest of the class.
- Be prepared to answer questions.
- Watch the other groups' presentations. Ask them questions about their courses.

D THINK ABOUT IT Take a class vote. Find out how many people are interested in each course.

Talk about adult education and career development

Café Hub

4.4 Busy day

F – ask for someone and leave a message   P – stress and intonation

COMPREHENSION

A Watch the video. Are the sentences true (T) or false (F)? Correct the false sentences.

1 Neena works in an office. T / F
2 Richard Sharp is busy. T / F
3 Neena's surname is Patel. T / F
4 She has to finish the Smith account today. T / F
5 She meets her mum for dinner. T / F
6 She usually finishes work at 10 pm. T / F
7 Neena wants a new job. T / F
8 She tells her mum about her new housemates. T / F

B Number the events in the order they happen. Then watch the video again and check.

Neena leaves a message for Richard Sharp.

Neena gets more work.

Neena gets started.

Lunchtime?

Neena speaks to her mum.

Finished?

FUNCTIONAL LANGUAGE

Asking for someone and leaving a message

A 00:00–01:37 Complete Neena's conversation with the receptionist. Then watch the first part of the video again and check.

Neena / **Receptionist**

Receptionist: Good [1] ___morning___. This is Morgan and Wise. Can I help?

Neena: Hello. [2] ____________ I speak to Richard Sharp, please?

Receptionist: Who's [3] ____________, please?

Neena: [4] ____________ Neena Patel.

Receptionist: Hold on a [5] ____________, please.

Receptionist: … I'm [6] ____________ he's not available at the moment. Would you like to [7] ____________ a message?

Neena: Yes, please. Can he call me [8] ____________?

Receptionist: Yes, what's your number?

Neena: It's 0207 946 0865.

B Work in pairs. Practice the conversation using your own name. Copy the stress and intonation.

MILLY

SAM

NEENA

ZAC

GABY

USEFUL PHRASES

Match the phrases (1–5) with their uses (a–e).

1 Hi, [mum]. It's me.
2 Right then,
3 Oh, dear.
4 Look,
5 Anyway,

a To change the subject.
b To react to bad news.
c To start a voicemail to someone you know.
d To make someone listen/understand.
e To begin a big or difficult job.

PRONUNCIATION

Stress and intonation

A 00:59–01:27 Watch part of Neena's conversation with the receptionist again. Notice the stress and intonation.

Neena:	Yes, please. Can he call me back?
Receptionist:	Yes, what's your number?
Neena:	It's 0207 946 0865.
Receptionist:	So, that's 0207 946 0865.
Neena:	Yes, that's right.

B 00:59–01:27 Watch again and repeat the conversation. Copy the stress and intonation.

Saying '0'

In British English, we usually say 'oh'.

In American English, we say 'oh' or 'zero'.

C Work in pairs. Practice the conversation in Exercise A, but change the phone number. Remember to use the correct stress and intonation.

Glossary

mum **(n) (British)** = mom **(n) (American)**
surname **(n) (British)** = last name **(n) (American)**

SPEAKING

A PLAN Work in pairs. Write a telephone conversation between yourself and a receptionist. Include these stages:

- You want to speak to a famous person.
- The famous person isn't available.
- You leave your name and number.

B PRACTICE Practice your conversation. Be careful with your stress and intonation.

C PRESENT Perform your conversation for the class.

A: Hello. Could I speak to Adele, please?
B: Who's speaking, please?

Ask for someone and leave a message

➤ Turn to page XXVII to learn how to write an email asking for information.

Unit 4 Review

VOCABULARY

A Complete the definitions with the jobs in the box.

dentist designer doctor hairdresser journalist mechanic pilot sales clerk

1 _______________ (n) a person that helps sick people
2 _______________ (n) a person that cuts people's hair
3 _______________ (n) a person that fixes cars
4 _______________ (n) a person that flies planes
5 _______________ (n) a person that fixes your teeth
6 _______________ (n) a person that works in a store
7 _______________ (n) a person that decides how something looks or works
8 _______________ (n) a person that reports the news

B Choose the correct words to complete the sentences.

1 In my country, teachers earn a good ***money / salary***.
2 My sister works ***full time / part time***. She's in the office three days a week.
3 I work for an electronics ***company / boss***.
4 My father's an actor. He's ***salary / self-employed***.
5 There are 200 ***colleagues / employees*** in the company.
6 My brother is a nurse. He works ***long hours / nine to five*** at night.

C Complete the sentences with the time expressions in the box.

early in the morning late in the afternoon noon midnight nine to five

1 The restaurant closes at 11 pm, so I usually don't get home until after _______________.
2 I have a normal office job. I work from _______________.
3 My wife starts work at 6 am, so she has to get up really _______________.
4 I have a meeting at _______________. Maybe we could go for lunch after that?
5 I work all night, so I sleep for most of the day. I usually don't get up until _______________.

D Complete the text with the words in the box.

course degree exam study train college

At the moment, I'm in my last year of school, but after that I want to go to [1]_______________. I want to [2]_______________ medicine, then [3]_______________ to be a doctor. I need to take an [4]_______________ at the end of this year before I can go to college and start my [5]_______________. It takes five years to complete the [6]_______________, and it's a lot of work – but it's my dream!

E SPEAK Work in pairs. Discuss the questions.

1 Do you have a degree? Do you want one?
2 Does anyone in your family go to college? Where? What do they study?
3 What would you like to take a course in?
4 How do you feel before an exam?

GRAMMAR

A Use the prompts to write *yes/no* questions then write short answers that are true for you.

1 you / work / outside?
Do you work outside? Yes, I do.
2 your colleagues / work / full time?
____
3 your company / make computers?
____
4 your boss / earn / a good salary?
____
5 you / like / your job?
____

B Complete the text with the correct form of *have to* and the verbs in parentheses.

My sister's a police officer in our hometown. She [1]_______________ (*work*) long hours, sometimes 10 or 12 hours a day, and she often [2]_______________ (*get up*) early, at 4 am. She [3]_______________ (*wear*) a blue uniform when she works outside, but when she's in the office, she [4]_______________ (*wear*) special clothes – she can wear her normal clothes. She and her colleagues often [5]_______________ (*help*) people in dangerous situations.

C Write questions to match the answers.

1 A: _______________
B: I live in a small apartment in the city center.
2 A: _______________
B: My teacher is Ms. Magnabosco.
3 A: _______________
B: I do my homework on the weekend.
4 A: _______________
B: My English course is two years.

FUNCTIONAL LANGUAGE

Complete the conversation with the words in the box.

call hang here message number speak that's

A: Hello?
B: Hi, it's Joe. Can I [1]_______________ to Maria, please?
A: She's not [2]_______________ at the moment.
B: Oh, right. Can I leave a [3]_______________?
A: [4]_______________ on a minute. I don't have a pen …
OK, I'm ready.
B: Can she [5]_______________ me back? My [6]_______________ is 800-555-0199.
A: OK, so [7]_______________ 800-555-0199.
B: That's right. Thanks!

5 PLACES

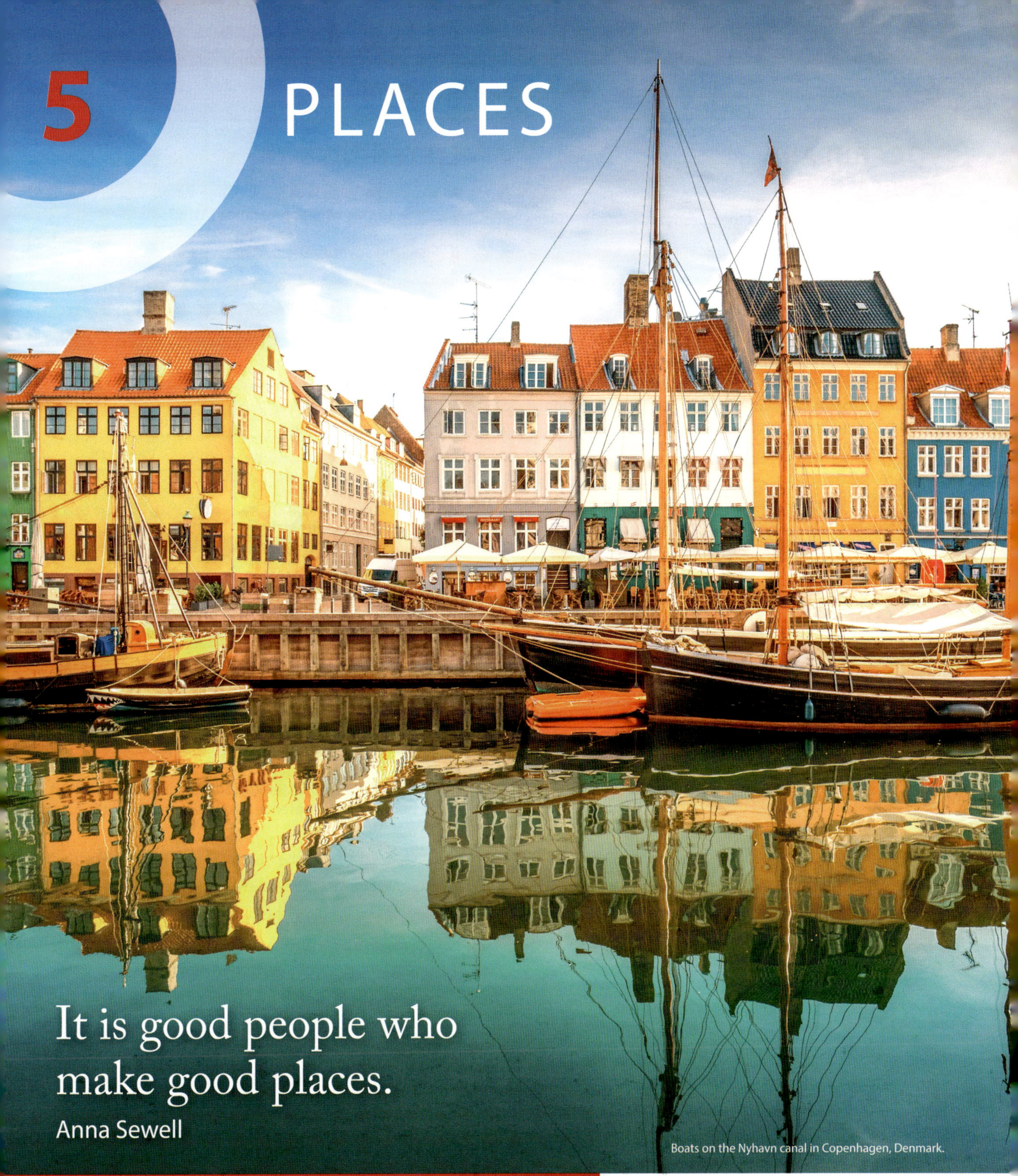

It is good people who make good places.

Anna Sewell

Boats on the Nyhavn canal in Copenhagen, Denmark.

OBJECTIVES

- describe a home
- describe a neighborhood
- describe an interesting building
- ask for and give directions
- write a description of a place

Work with a partner. Discuss the questions.

1 Where do you live?
2 Look at the picture. Would you like to live there? Why/Why not?
3 What's your favorite city?

5.1 There's no place like home

Describe a home

V rooms and furniture; prepositions of place **P** /b/, /d/ and /g/ **G** *there is/are*

VOCABULARY

Rooms and furniture

A Work in pairs and discuss the questions.

1 Do you live in a house or an apartment?
2 Who do you live with?
3 How many rooms are there?
4 Where do you spend most of your time?

B Go to the **Vocabulary Hub** on **page XX**.

C **SPEAK** Work in pairs. Student A – imagine you are in a room in your house or apartment. Describe what you can see. Student B – guess which room your partner is talking about.

A: I can see a TV and a lamp.
B: You're in the living room!
A: No, I'm in the bedroom!

PRONUNCIATION

/b/, /d/ and /g/

5.1 **A** The words below all begin with /b/, /d/ or /g/ sounds. Listen and repeat.

/b/	/d/	/g/
bedroom	dining	garden
bathroom	don't	go
brother	day	grow

5.2 **B** Listen and write the words in the correct place in Exercise A.

5.3 **C** Listen, check and repeat.

LISTENING

A Work in pairs. Look at the pictures. Where would you prefer to stay when on vacation? Why?

B Read the advertisement. What is it for?

5.4 **C** **LISTEN FOR GIST** Listen to Sadie talking to Luke about his house. Which sentence (1–3) best describes their conversation?

1 Sadie doesn't like the house.
2 Sadie and Luke agree to swap houses.
3 Sadie doesn't understand the house swap rules.

5.4 **D** **LISTEN FOR KEY WORDS** Listen again. Choose the correct words to complete the sentences.

1 Sadie is from the south of *France* / *England*.
2 Luke's caravan has *two* / *three* beds.
3 Luke's caravan *has* / *doesn't have* a swimming pool.
4 Luke's caravan *has four* / *doesn't have any* chairs.
5 Sadie *has* / *doesn't have* a house.

E **SPEAK** Work in pairs. What do you like about Luke's home? What don't you like?

GRAMMAR
there is/are

A WORK IT OUT Read three parts of Luke and Sadie's conversation. Complete the table using the conversation as an example.

1

Sadie: Uh … yes. So, are there any beds in your house?

Luke: Beds? Yes, there are. There are two beds. There's a bed in the bedroom and another bed across from the kitchen.

2

Sadie: I see. Is there a swimming pool?

Luke: … No, there isn't a swimming pool.

3

Sadie: OK … Well, are there any chairs in the dining room?

Luke: No, there aren't any chairs.

there is/are		
	Singular	Plural
Positive +	There[1] _'s_ a dining room.	There [2] ________ two bathrooms.
Negative -	There [3] ________ a TV.	There [4] ________ any plants.
Questions ?	[5] ________ a dishwasher?	[6] ________ any chairs?

some* and *any

We use *some* in positive sentences with plural nouns.

We use *any* in questions and negative sentences with plural nouns.

A: *Are there any armchairs?*

B: *No, there aren't any armchairs, but there are some chairs.*

B Go to the **Grammar Hub** on **page XIV**.

C SPEAK Work in pairs. Ask your partner about their home using some of the words in the box.

armchair bathtub coffee machine cupboard fridge lamp plant shower sink couch table TV dishwasher window

A: Are there any lamps in your living room?
B: No, there aren't. But there is a lamp in the bedroom. Is there a dishwasher in your kitchen?
A: Yes, there is.

VOCABULARY
Prepositions of place

Look at the pictures of Luke's caravan. Match sentences (1–5) to objects (a–e).

1 They're **in** the small cupboard **near** the coffee machine.
2 They're **behind** the lamp.
3 It's **under** the window, **between** the plant and the wall.
4 They're **on** the small table, **across from** the couch.
5 It's **next to** the kitchen sink.

a coffee machine
b bed
c books
d keys
e TV and DVD player

SPEAKING

A Imagine you have a vacation home. Where is it?

B PLAN Write notes about your vacation home. Think about these questions:

- What type of home is it?
- How many rooms are there?
- Does it have a big or small kitchen?
- Is there a yard or swimming pool?

C PREPARE Write an advertisement for a house swap.

D SPEAK Work in groups. Read each other's ads. Ask questions and decide who you want to swap with.

Describe a home

5.2 My neighborhood

Describe a neighborhood

V places in a town or city G *can* P weak forms: *can/can't*

VOCABULARY

Places in a town or city

A SPEAK Work in pairs. Which of the sentences (1–3) best describes you?

1 I like quiet areas away from the center of the city.

2 I like busy areas in the city, with lots of people and stores.

3 I don't like the city. I like small towns and the countryside.

B Work in pairs. Look at the pictures. Which of the places in the box can you see?

café movie theater gym hospital library market museum park stores grocery store theater

C Go to the **Vocabulary Hub** on **page XX**.

D SPEAK Work in pairs. Which of the places in Exercise B or in the Vocabulary are there in your neighborhood? Which would you like to have?

In my neighborhood, there's a grocery store, but there aren't any small stores.

READING

A READ FOR GIST Read the comments in the *Chicago Expats* forum. Who is Grace and what is her problem?

B READ FOR SPECIFIC INFORMATION Read the comments again and answer the questions.

1 Where is Grace from?

2 Where is Grace's new job?

3 Which two places can she go to in Jackson Park?

4 What does Grace like doing?

5 Where is the gym?

6 How far is Hyde Park from the center of Chicago?

C SPEAK Work in pairs. Do you think Hyde Park is a good place for Grace to live? Why/Why not?

Chicago Expats

amazinggrace26: Hi, people of Chicago! My name's Grace. I'm 26 and I'm a nurse in the Philippines. I have a new job at the University Hospital in Hyde Park, and I'm a little nervous because this is my first time abroad. Can you tell me something about the neighborhood? What is there to do in Hyde Park? I like warm weather, and my hobbies are reading and keeping fit.

Yesterday, 08:39 Reply | Like

Marco: Hi Grace. I work at the University Hospital, too. There are a lot of things you can do in Hyde Park. There are some good restaurants and cafés, and Jackson Park nearby is really nice. Can you play tennis? There are some very good tennis courts in Jackson Park. There's even a science museum there, too!

Yesterday, 12:21 Reply | Like

amazinggrace26: Thanks, Marco. It sounds great. I can't play tennis, but I'd like to learn! And the museum sounds wonderful! Is there a gym at the hospital? I like to swim and keep fit.

Yesterday, 15:05 Reply | Like

Marco: There isn't a gym at the hospital, but there is one very close to it. And it's cheap for people who work at the hospital 😃

Yesterday, 17:12 Reply | Like

helen264: Hi, Grace. Hyde Park is nice, but for me, it can be boring. I prefer the city center – it's only 20 minutes away. You can go to the theater, stores and to see a movie. Sorry, but I can't promise you good weather! Chicago is often cold!

Today, 09:45 Reply | Like

amazinggrace26: Thanks for your advice, @Helen264. I feel really excited about Chicago now!

Glossary

expat (n) someone who lives in a country that is not their own

GRAMMAR

can

A WORK IT OUT Read the sentences from the *Chicago Expats* forum. Then choose the correct words to complete the rules.

Can you play tennis?	… it can be boring.
You can go to the theater …	I can't play tennis …

can

1 We use *can* to talk about ***ability and possibility / the past***.
2 In positive and negative sentences, *can* comes ***before / after*** the main verb.
3 We use the ***infinitive / base form*** after *can*.
4 We ***use / don't use*** questions that start with *Do …?*
5 We ***add / don't add*** -s in the third person.

B Go to the **Grammar Hub** on **page XIV**.

C SPEAK Work in pairs. Ask each other questions starting with *Can you …?* Use the ideas below to help you.

- arrive at work when you want
- go to the movie theater in your neighborhood
- play a musical instrument
- play tennis
- speak another language
- swim
- work from home

A: Can you arrive at work when you want?
B: I don't work, but I can usually arrive at the university when I want. Can you play soccer?

PRONUNCIATION

Weak forms: *can/can't*

5.5 **A** Listen and read. What do you notice about the pronunciation of *can* and *can't*?

1 Can you speak another language?
2 Yes, I can. I can speak Italian fluently.
3 No, I can't. I'm not very good at languages.
4 I can speak a little French, but I can't speak it very well.

5.5 **B** Listen again and repeat the sentences. Copy the pronunciation of *can* and *can't*.

SPEAKING

A PREPARE Imagine you want to move to a new neighborhood. Work with a partner to rank questions (a–g) from 1 (very important) to 8 (not important).

a What are the people like? ___
b Are there any good schools? ___
c What's the weather like? ___
d How far is it from the airport? ___
e What's in the city center? ___
f Are there any good stores? ___
g Is there a train station? ___

A: It's important for me to be close to my family and friends.
B: Yes, that's a good point. And public transportation is important to me.

B ORGANIZE What can you do in your neighborhood? Write notes.

C SPEAK Work in pairs. Imagine your partner is interested in moving to your neighborhood. Describe it to them, explaining what is good and bad about the area.

There are a lot of stores, but there aren't any parks.

D SPEAK Ask questions about your partner's neighborhood. Decide if you want to move there.

Describe a neighborhood

5.3 Amazing buildings

Describe an interesting building

G imperatives V adjectives to describe the appearance of things P word stress: adjectives
S reading for specific information

READING

A Look at the famous buildings (1–5) in *The world's most interesting buildings*. What do you know about them? Do you know where they are?

B **READ FOR GIST** Read *The world's most interesting buildings*. Match pictures (1–5) with paragraphs (a–d). There is one picture you do not need.

1

C Read the article again. In which building(s) can you do these things? Use the information in the box to help you.

Reading for specific information

- Read the text quickly and look for keywords that help you find the information you're looking for.
- For example, if you want to know about prices or times, look for numbers. Then read around them to find the information.

1 have lunch ________

2 see art ________

3 swim ________

4 work ________

5 live ________

D **SPEAK** Work in pairs. Which building is your favorite? Which building don't you like? Why?

The world's *most interesting buildings*

What happens when you mix buildings and art? Read on and find out! This week's topic in *Architecture Online* is the world's most **interesting** and original buildings. These are our favorite buildings. Tell us which ones you like.

a This **strange** building isn't falling down! It's the Dancing House, in Prague, Czech Republic. It's **funny**! There are offices in the building, and there's a restaurant on the top floor. Look at how many windows there are! Some people don't like the Dancing House because it's next to a lot of old buildings in a historic part of the city on a busy road. They think it's **terrible**. _____

2

b These yellow and white buildings that look like trees are Piet Blom's Cube Houses in Rotterdam, the Netherlands. They are **tall** and **beautiful**. The living rooms are downstairs and the bedrooms are on the top floor. Some houses have a yard on the roof. _____

c This **amazing** house looks very **old**, but it isn't. In fact, it's only 40 years old. It's *Casa do Penedo*, or 'Stone House' in Portugal. The **small** house sits between four **big** rocks. There's a swimming pool in one of the rocks. You can visit the house because it's a local history museum. _____

d This is the Niterói Contemporary Art Museum in Rio de Janeiro, Brazil. It's an art gallery and a museum. The building is next to a beach and has views of Rio and the Sugarloaf Mountain. The museum is very popular with tourists. We think this **modern** building is **cool**. _____

3

GRAMMAR
Imperatives

A WORK IT OUT Look at the sentences from *The world's most interesting buildings*. Then choose the correct words to complete the rules.

Read on and **find** out!

Tell us which ones you like.

Imperatives

1 We use imperatives when we want to ***tell someone to do something / talk about the future***.
2 We use the ***infinitive / base form*** to make imperatives.
3 We ***can / can't*** use *please* with imperatives.

B Find and underline one more imperative in *The world's most interesting buildings*.

C Go to the **Grammar Hub** on **page XIV**.

D SPEAK Work in pairs. Use the verbs in the box to make imperative sentences. Remember to say *please*.

give lend sit down spell stand up tell write

Stand up, please.

VOCABULARY
Adjectives to describe the appearance of things

A Look at the adjectives in **bold** in *The world's most interesting buildings*. Which are positive? Which are negative? Which are neutral?

Positive: ______

Negative: ______

Neutral: ______

B Match adjectives (1–5) with their opposites (a–e).

1 beautiful	a boring
2 interesting	b old
3 amazing	c small
4 big	d terrible
5 modern	e ugly

C SPEAK Work in pairs. Describe an interesting building in your neighborhood using adjectives from Exercise B.

There's a new shopping center in the middle of town. It's a big, modern building with lots of windows.

PRONUNCIATION
Word stress: adjectives

5.6 **A** Listen and repeat. Copy the word stress.

●•	●••
boring	*beautiful*

5.7 **B** Complete the table in Exercise A with the words in the box. Then listen and check.

~~beautiful~~ ~~boring~~ building funny gallery interesting modern popular terrible ugly

5.7 **C** Listen again and repeat the words. Copy the word stress.

SPEAKING HUB

A SPEAK Work in pairs. Go to the **Communication Hub** on **page XXIII**.

B DISCUSS Work in groups. Discuss the questions.

1 Which of the buildings in the Communication Hub is your favorite? Why?
2 What's your favorite building in your country? Why do you like it?
3 Do you think it's important for buildings to look interesting? Why/Why not?

C Take a class vote on the most interesting building.

Describe an interesting building

Café Hub

5.4 Moving in

F – ask for and give directions   P – stress and intonation

COMPREHENSION

A Watch the video without sound. Check (✓) the items you see.

☐ café	☐ library
☐ chair	☐ park
☐ cinema	☐ plant
☐ fridge	☐ sofa
☐ gym	☐ supermarket
☐ house	☐ table
☐ lamp	☐ theater

B **SPEAK** Work in pairs. Ask questions to check your answers to Exercise A.

A: Is there a gym?
B: No, there isn't. Is there a café?
A: I'm not sure …

C Watch the video with sound and choose the correct option to complete the sentences.

1 Gaby *gets* / *doesn't get* cash.
2 Gaby *loses* / *doesn't lose* her phone.
3 Gaby *has to* / *doesn't have to* ask for directions twice.
4 Gaby *can* / *can't* find her door key.
5 Gaby *spends* / *doesn't spend* the evening with Neena.

FUNCTIONAL LANGUAGE

Asking for and giving directions

A Label pictures (1–4) with the directions in the box.

Go straight ahead | Turn right | Turn right at the café | Turn left

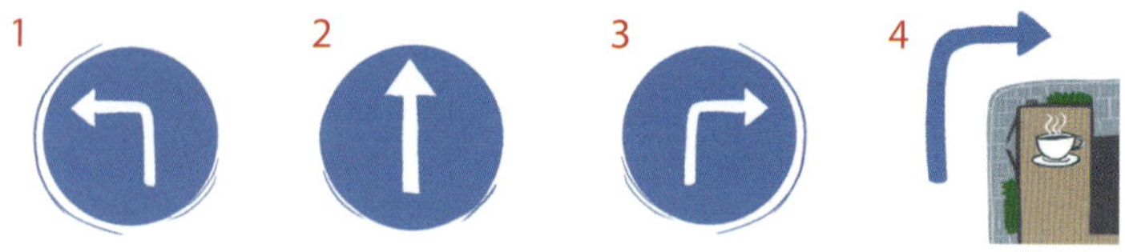

1 ________ 2 ________ 3 ________ 4 ________

B Match the directions in the box to images (1–4).

Asking for directions	Excuse me, is there a cash machine near here? Excuse me, can you tell me the way to Park Road?
Giving directions	__ Go straight ahead to the end of the road. __ Go past the stores. __ Take the third turn on the left. __ The cash machine is next to the supermarket.

C **SPEAK** Work in pairs. Take turns giving directions from your school to:

- a cash machine
- a train station
- a coffee shop

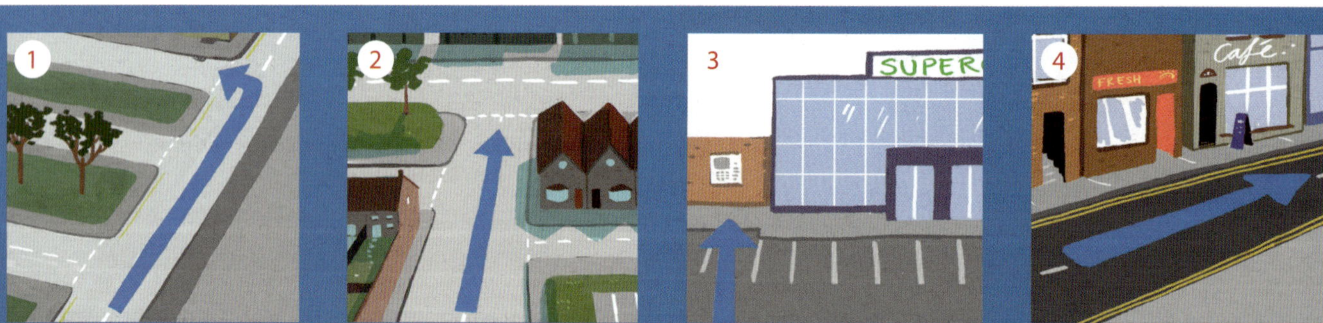

Glossary

cinema **(n) (British)** = movie theater **(n) (American)**
sofa **(n) (British)** = couch **(n) (American)**
door key **(n) (British)** = house key **(n) (American)**

MILLY

SAM

NEENA

ZAC

GABY

PRONUNCIATION

Stress and intonation

A 00:00–00:47 Watch the first part of the video again. Listen to the conversation between Gaby and the passer-by. Notice the stress and intonation.

Gaby: Excuse me, is there a cash machine near here?

Passer-by: Sure. Go straight on to the end of the road. Turn right at the café. And the cash machine is next to the supermarket.

B 00:00–00:47 Watch again and repeat the conversation. Copy the stress and intonation.

C **SPEAK** Work in pairs. Practice the conversation in Exercise A. Remember to use the correct stress and intonation.

SPEAKING

DISCUSS Work in pairs. Ask for and give directions using the map. Use some of the Functional language and the prepositions in the box to help you.

behind | between | near | next to | on

A: Excuse me. Is there a school near here?

B: Sure, take the second turn on the left.

Ask for and give directions

➤ Turn to page XXVIII to learn how to write a description of a place.

Unit 5 Review

GRAMMAR

A Match the beginnings of sentences (1–5) with the ends of sentences (a–e).

1 There's — c
2 There aren't
3 Are there
4 Is there
5 There are

a a table in the kitchen?
b some cupboards in the bathroom.
c a shower in the bathroom.
d any lamps in the sitting room?
e any chairs in the dining room.

B Complete the conversation with the correct form of *can*.

Simon: [1] ___Can___ you ride a motorcycle?
Patrick: No, I [2] ________, but I [3] ________ drive a car. Do you want a ride?
Simon: [4] ________ we walk to the park from here?
Patrick: Well, we [5] ________, but it takes a long time.

C Choose the correct words to complete the sentences.

1 *Tell* / *To tell* me more about the Colosseum in Rome.
2 *Look* / *Looking* at the tourists.
3 *Please give* / *Give please* me more information.
4 *Ask* / *To Ask* at the front desk for more information.
5 *Write* / *Wrote* about your favorite building.

VOCABULARY

A Complete the furniture and rooms with *a*, *e*, *i*, *o* or *u*.

1 We have a sh_o_w_e_r, but we don't have a b_a_tht_u_b in our b_a_thr_o_ _o_m.
2 We have a modern __v__n and fr__dg__ in our k__tch__n.
3 There's a TV, a big c__pb__ __rd, a c__ __ch and two __rmch__ __rs in our sitting room.
4 There's a l__mp on the t__bl__ by my bed in my b__dr__ __m.

B Look at the picture. Choose the correct prepositions to complete the sentences.

1 The coffee machine is *between* / *next to* the oven and the sink.
2 The house keys are hanging *on* / *in* the wall.
3 The dishwasher is *next to* / *behind* the oven.
4 The note is *above* / *under* the window.

C Complete the sentences with the places in the box.

airport gym ~~hospital~~ library market

1 You see a doctor at the ___hospital___.
2 You take a plane at the ________.
3 You borrow a book from the ________.
4 You buy fresh food at a ________.
5 You exercise at the ________.

D Complete the text with the correct adjectives.

My favorite building is Habitat 67, in Montréal, Quebec. It's [1]a_m_ _a_ _z_ _i_ _n_g – it's [2]b__g and looks very [3]m__ __ __ __n, even though it's 50 years old. It isn't one building, it's about 150 [4]s__ __ __l houses on top of each other. Some people think it looks [5]s__ __ __ __ __e, but I think it's [6]b__ __ __ __ __ __ __ __l. You can see the sky through it, which is [7]c__ __l.

FUNCTIONAL LANGUAGE

A Complete the conversation with the words in the box.

down ~~excuse~~ here how on tell turn (x2)

A: [1] ___Excuse___ me.
B: Yes?
A: Can you [2] ________ me the way to New Street?
B: Sorry?
A: Is New Street near [3] ________?
B: Excuse me?
A: [4] ________ do I get to New Street?
B: Oh, yes. Go [5] ________ College Road. [6] ________ right onto High Street and Moon Street is [7] ________ your right.
A: Moon Street? I want New Street.
B: New Street? No, no. New Street is near here. Take the second [8] ________ on the right.
A: Oh, thanks.

B SPEAK Work in pairs. Give each other directions from your school to:

- a bookstore
- a train station
- a museum

6 THAT'S ENTERTAINMENT

If music be the food of love, play on.

William Shakespeare

An actor on stage in the Théâtre du Châtelet in Paris, France.

OBJECTIVES

- talk about likes and dislikes
- talk about entertainment in the present and the past
- talk about your life
- ask for and give opinions
- review an event

Work with a partner. Discuss the questions.

1 What's your favorite kind of music?
2 Look at the picture. What's he doing?
3 How often do you go to the movie theater?

6.1 Let's go out

Talk about likes and dislikes

V entertainment **P** word stress: noun patterns **G** likes and dislikes

VOCABULARY

Entertainment

A Match pictures (1–6) with the places and events (a–f).

a a comedy show	___	**d** a concert	___
b an exhibit	___	**e** a festival	___
c a movie theater	___	**f** a theater	___

B SPEAK Work with a partner. How often do you go to the places and events in Exercise A?

PRONUNCIATION

Word stress: noun patterns

6.1 **A** Listen and repeat the words. Copy the word stress.

movie comedy concert exhibit
festival internet magazine

6.2 **B** Complete the table with the words from Exercise A. Then listen, check and repeat.

●•	●••	••●	•●•

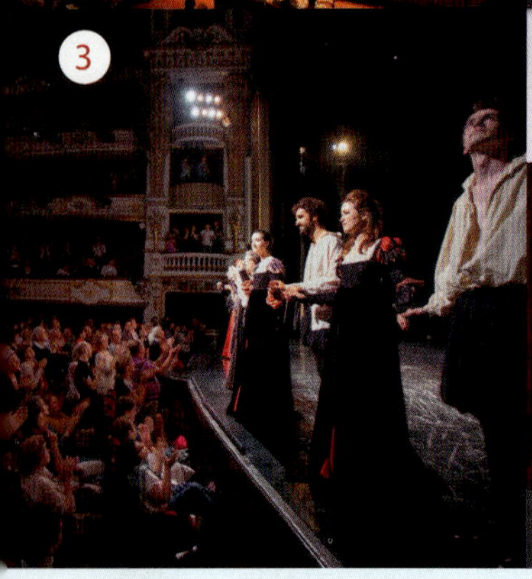

READING

A Read the *City Guide*. Check (✓) the information you can get from it.

- ☐ the date of an event
- ☐ how much an event costs
- ☐ what time the events start/finish
- ☐ how often the event happens
- ☐ how to get to an event
- ☐ where an event is
- ☐ the writer's opinion of an event
- ☐ things to do in October

City Guide

What's going on?

Today | **This week** | This weekend

Things to do this week (August 10 – 16)
No plans this week? Well, not anymore. We're here to help! From movies to festivals, here's your guide to the next seven days. Let's go out!

Star Wars ★★★★★
Watch the first three *Star Wars* movies, a different movie each evening over three nights. Saturday is a special family day when you can wear costumes.
Langley Outdoor Movie Theater, 6 pm, from Thursday, August 13

Cow ★★★
Californian rock band, Cow, often play in strange locations. This Friday, their concert is in an old swimming pool. Enjoy some old favorites and songs from their new album.
The Old Baths, 9 pm, Friday, August 14

Comedy Underground ★★★★
For one night, comedians Lily O'Connor and Josh Peet take their new show underground. That's right – two hours of free comedy as you travel on the subway!
City Line, 8 pm – 10 pm, Thursday, August 13

Kwame Abraham ★★★★★
This exhibit of Kwame Abraham's photographs shows people from his country, Ghana, during the 1960s. His images tell amazing stories.
The Hayforth Gallery, 10 am – 9:30 pm, Wednesday, August 12 – Sunday, September 6

Glossary

comedian (n) someone who tells jokes and stories to make people laugh
free (adj) something that doesn't cost anything
costume (n) clothes that performers wear in a play, movie, etc
location (n) where something is or where something happens
silent (adj) not making any noise

B READ FOR SPECIFIC INFORMATION Read the guide again. Complete the sentences with no more than three words from the text.

1 The Kwame Abraham exhibit finishes on ____________.
2 The music festival lasts for ____________ days.
3 The Star Wars event starts at ____________ on Thursday August 13.
4 Cow's performance is in a ____________ in The Old Baths.
5 James Cave is ____________ in the performance of *Romeo and Juliet*.

Search

Silent disco ★★★★
The silent disco craze continues! Put on your headphones, choose any kind of music and dance to your favorite tunes.
Nanette's, 10 pm – 5 am, Saturday, August 15

Lost in the Forest Festival ★★★★
A three-day music festival with great food and dancing under the tall, green trees of Coney Forest.
Coney Forest, Friday – Sunday, August 14 – 16

Shakespeare in the park ★★★
Tonight's play is *Romeo and Juliet*, Shakespeare's famous love story. With James Cave as Romeo and Ameera Hussain as Juliet. Bring warm clothes and a picnic.
Linkside Park, 6 pm, Tuesday, August 11

C How do you know which events the *What's going on?* guide recommends? Which events have four- (★★★★) or five-star (★★★★★) ratings?

D SPEAK Work in pairs. How do you find events?

online apps newspaper magazine friends family social media

I find events on an app on my phone. I go to pop-up events all the time.

GRAMMAR
Likes and dislikes

A (6.3) Listen to Dan and Lucy planning a night out. Which events in the *What's going on?* guide do they talk about? What do they decide to do?

B (6.3) Complete the sentences from the conversation with the words in the box. Then listen again and check your answers.

don't like (x2) hate like love

1 **Dan:** I ____________ staying in on Friday night. Let's go out.
2 **Dan:** It's that rock band from California, Cow. I ____________ their music.
3 **Lucy:** Sorry, I don't really like them. I ____________ rock music.
4 **Lucy:** I ____________ sitting outside. It's too cold.
5 **Dan:** You ____________ photography, don't you?

C WORK IT OUT Look at the sentences in Exercise B. Complete the rules with *noun* or *verb*.

Likes and dislikes

1 We use *like, love, don't like* and *hate* + ____________
2 We use *like, love, don't like* and *hate* + ____________ + *-ing*.

D Go to the **Grammar Hub** on **page XVI**.

E SPEAK Work in small groups. Discuss the questions.

1 What do you like doing in your free time?
2 What kind of events do you love? Which do you hate? Why?
3 What do you like doing on your birthday?
4 Do you like going to outdoor events (e.g. festivals, outdoor movie theaters, etc)? Why/Why not?

SPEAKING

A PREPARE Work in pairs and discuss what you *like, love, don't like* and *hate* in the *What's going on?* guide.

B SPEAK Go to the **Communication Hub** on **page XXII**.

Talk about likes and dislikes

6.2 It was fun

Talk about entertainment in the present and the past

G *was/were* **P** weak forms: *was/were* **V** past time expressions

1 ______________________

2 ______________________

3 ______________________

4 ______________________

LISTENING

A Work in pairs. Label the pictures (1–4) with the time periods in the box.

1930s 1950s 1980s 2000s

6.4 **B LISTEN FOR KEY WORDS** Listen to Carrie and her grandfather talking about TV. Check (✓) the things that they talk about.

TV channels	☐	laptops and tablets	☐
movie night	☐	TV dinners	☐
TV on demand	☐	an old TV show	☐

6.4 **C LISTEN FOR DETAIL** Listen to the conversation again. Are the sentences true (T) or false (F)? Correct the false sentences.

1 Carrie can't watch the nature show. *T / F*
2 Carrie watches her favorite TV show on demand. *T / F*
3 Carrie's grandfather's favorite TV show was on once a week. *T / F*
4 When Carrie's grandfather was young, there were a lot of TV channels. *T / F*
5 TVs weren't expensive in the 1950s. *T / F*
6 Carrie's grandfather thinks families today don't do things together. *T / F*

D SPEAK Work in pairs. Answer the questions.

1 What are your favorite TV shows?
2 Do you watch them with friends and family or alone?
3 How often do you watch shows on demand?

GRAMMAR

was/were

A Read the sentences from the conversation between Carrie and her grandpa. Underline the verbs.

1 They were expensive.
2 There weren't many TV channels.
3 Was that nice, Grandpa?
4 I wasn't lonely.
5 It was fun.

B WORK IT OUT Look at Exercise A. Complete the rules with *was*, *wasn't*, *were* or *weren't*.

was/were

1 ______________ is the past form of *is*.
______________ is the past form of *are*.

2 ______________ is the past form of *isn't*.
______________ is the past form of *aren't*.

3 We make *yes/no* questions with ______________ or ______________ + subject.

C Go to the **Grammar Hub** on **page XVI**.

D SPEAK Ask *Where were you …?* using the times below.

- at 11 pm last night
- at 10 am on Saturday morning
- at 6 pm on Friday
- at 2 pm yesterday
- at 8 am this morning

Where were you at 11 pm last night?

PRONUNCIATION
Weak forms: *was/were*

6.5 **A** Listen and read. What do you notice about the pronunciation of *was* and *were*?

1 When I was young, my favorite TV show was on once a week.
2 How many TV channels were there?
3 Yes, they were.
4 Was that nice, Grandpa?
5 Yes, it was. I wasn't lonely. People did things together. It was fun.

6.5 **B** Underline the weak forms of *was* and *were* in Exercise A. Then listen again and check.

C Work in pairs. Practice saying the sentences in Exercise A. Remember to use the correct forms of *was* and *were*.

VOCABULARY
Past time expressions

A Work in pairs to complete the *Big screen, small screen* quiz.

B Use the words in the box to make a table of past time expressions. Some words can go in more than one place.

10 minutes 1952 Friday June month six weeks two years weekend winter year

in	ago	last

C Complete the sentences with *in*, *ago*, *last* or *yesterday*.

1 I was in Mexico _______________ year.
2 Our exams were exactly one year _______________.
3 I wasn't at home _______________ July. I was on vacation.
4 I was a student two months _______________. Now I have a job!
5 My parents were students _______________ 1982.
6 I was at home with my family _______________.

D SPEAK Work in pairs. Ask and answer questions beginning with *Where were you ...?* Use the table in Exercise B to help you.

A: Where were you last month?
B: I was in Istanbul last month. Where were you at this time yesterday?
A: I was in this class!

SPEAKING

A PREPARE Write five questions about entertainment now and in the past. Use time expressions in your questions.

What's your favorite TV show?
What was your favorite movie ten years ago?

B SPEAK Work in pairs. Ask and answer the questions in Exercise A.

five/ten/twenty years ago in the 80s/90s last year

A: What were your favorite TV shows ten years ago?
B: My favorite TV show 10 years ago was ...

BIG SCREEN, SMALL SCREEN

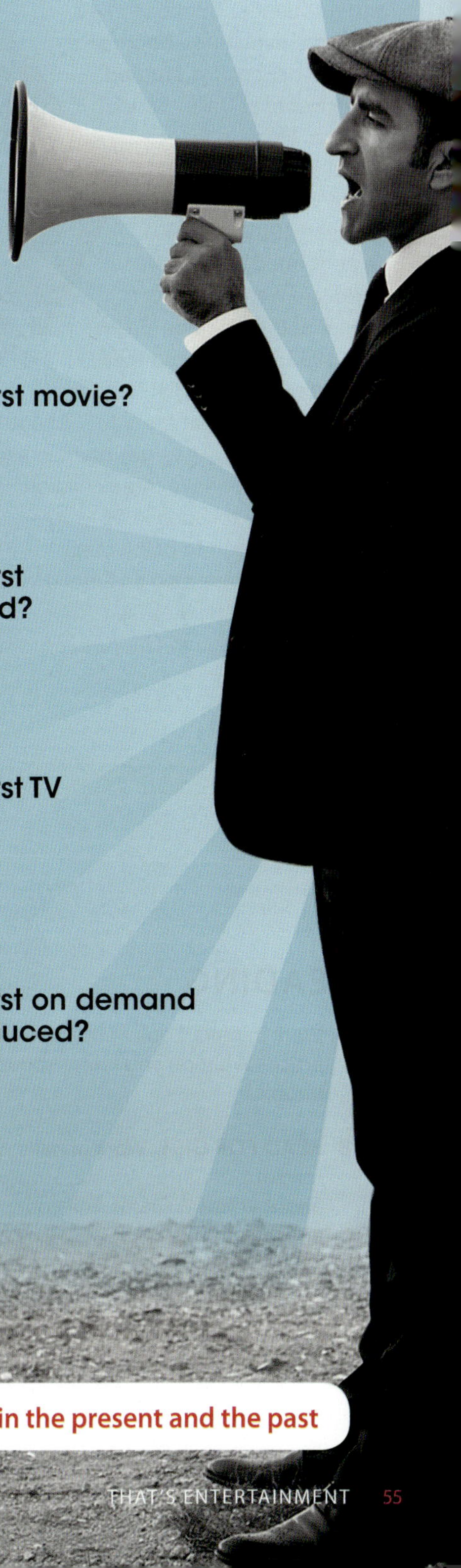

1 When was the first movie?
a in the 1850s
b in the 1880s
c in the 1900s

2 When was the first movie with sound?
a in the 1910s
b in the 1920s
c in the 1930s

3 When was the first TV introduced?
a 90 years ago
b 70 years ago
c 50 years ago

4 When was the first on demand TV service introduced?
a last year
b this century
c last century

Talk about entertainment in the present and the past

G simple past regular and irregular verbs P simple past regular endings V life events S scanning for names

Entertainer Magazine
Inspiring stories

Carlos Acosta
by Helena Nowak

Carlos Acosta was born into a large, poor family in Havana, Cuba, in 1973. When he was nine years old, his father, Pedros Acosta, **sent** him to dance school. At first, he hated it – he just wanted to play soccer with his friends. But he worked hard and, eventually, **became** a talented dancer. He **studied** at the National Ballet School of Cuba. He won the gold medal at the Prix de Lausanne.
Between 1989 and 1991, he performed around the world. He was a principal dancer at the Houston Ballet from 1993 to 1998, and then he **started** a new job at London's Royal Ballet. He met his wife, Charlotte Holland, in 2004. They **got** married eight years later. They have three children. He **went** back to Cuba in 2011 to start a foundation to help young dancers. Acosta is also an actor. He appeared in the movies *New York, I Love You* (2008) and *Our Kind of Traitor* (2016).

Venus Williams
by Nao Yamauchi

Venus Williams was born in Lynwood, near Compton in Los Angeles, in 1980. There was a lot of crime in the local area and her father, Richard Williams, thought tennis was a chance for Venus and her younger sister Serena to be rich and successful.
The Williams sisters **played** tennis on old courts. They **practiced** with tennis balls from nearby country clubs. Their father was their coach, and their mother, Oracene Price, **gave** them school lessons at home. When she was ten, Venus **moved** to Florida where she went to Rick Macci's tennis academy. Before she was a teenager, she won 63 matches without losing one.
In February 2002, Venus Williams became the first African American to be the world's number one tennis player. In July of the same year, Venus played Serena in the Wimbledon final, and Serena won and became world number one. These sisters, from a poor neighborhood in Los Angeles, are now recognized as two of the greatest female tennis players in the world.

Glossary

inspiring (adj) making you feel excited about something

READING

A Work in pairs. Look at the pictures in the article. What do you know about these people?

B **READ FOR GIST** Work in pairs. Student A – read about Carlos Acosta. Student B – read about Venus Williams. Tell your partner about your person.

C **READ FOR DETAIL** Read the article again and complete the sentences with names from the text. Use the information in the box to help you.

Scanning for names

- When scanning for names of people or places, look for CAPITAL LETTERS.
- When scanning for names of movies, albums and books, look for *italics*.

1 ____________ wanted Venus and Serena to learn tennis.
2 Carlos got married to ____________.
3 In 2008, Carlos was in a movie called ____________.
4 Venus moved to ____________ in 1990.
5 ____________ sent Carlos to dance school for the first time.
6 ____________ became world number one in July 2002.
7 Carlos got a gold medal from ____________.
8 ____________ helped Venus with school lessons at home.

D **SPEAK** Work in pairs. Which person inspires you? Why?

A: I like Carlos Acosta because he helps young dancers.
B: I think Venus is more inspiring. She was the first African American to be the world's number one tennis player.

GRAMMAR

Simple past regular and irregular verbs

A WORK IT OUT Read *Inspiring stories* again. Complete the table with past verbs from the article.

Simple past regular and irregular verbs			
Regular		**Irregular**	
move	________	become	________
play	________	get	________
practice	________	go	________
start	________	give	________
study	________	send	________

B Look at the rules about simple past regular verbs. Check (✓) the rules that are true.

Simple past regular verbs

1 ☐ We add *-ed* to most verbs.
2 ☐ We add *-d* to verbs ending in *-e*.
3 ☐ We add *-s* to the third person.
4 ☐ With verbs ending in *-y*, we drop the *-y* and add *-ied*.

C See the **Irregular verbs** list on **page XXX**.

D Go to the **Grammar Hub** on **page XVI**.

E SPEAK Work in pairs. Tell your partner three things you did last year.

A: I went to Greece, I bought a new laptop and I passed my English exam! What about you?
B: Good job! I joined a gym, I met my best friend and I started college.

PRONUNCIATION

Simple past regular endings

6.6 **A** There are three different ways of pronouncing the endings of simple past regular verbs. Can you hear the difference? Listen and repeat.

/d/	/t/	/ɪd/
died	liked	waited

6.7 **B** Listen and add the verbs in the box to the table in Exercise A.

asked decided moved stopped studied wanted worked

6.7 **C** Listen again and repeat the verbs.

VOCABULARY

Life events

A Complete the phrases with the verbs in the box. Use the words in bold in *Inspiring stories* to help you.

be become get go have move start study

1 ________ married
2 ________ a dancer/musician/singer
3 ________ to school/college
4 ________ work
5 ________ art / a language
6 ________ born
7 ________ children
8 ________ to a different city/house

B SPEAK Put the life events in Exercise A in the order that you think they happen. Then work in pairs. Are your life events in the same order? Can you think of any other life events?

A: What about learning to drive? That's a big life event for most people.
B: That's true. I learned to drive when I was 17. It really changed my life!

SPEAKING HUB

A PREPARE You are going to write about your life. Think about how to complete the sentences.

- I was born in …
- I went …
- I studied …
- I started …
- I moved …
- I got married to …
- I had …
- I lived in …
- I worked in …

B PLAN Choose the five most important events in your life. Write each one on a separate piece of paper and then fold it in half.

C ORGANIZE Work in groups. Put all of your sentences in the middle. Take turns reading sentences aloud and guessing who wrote them. Award one point for every correct guess.

I graduated from Bologna University.

It's Francesca's sentence!

D DISCUSS Work in groups. Try to remember the events of other people's lives.

Sayeed studied English in Australia.

Yes, and Ana got married last month!

Talk about your life

Café Hub

6.4 Love hate

F– ask for and give opinions P– stress and intonation

COMPREHENSION

A 00:00–00:56 **SPEAK** Work in pairs. Watch the first part of the video. What is Zac's big news?

B 00:56–03:57 Watch the second part of the video and complete the table. Draw ☺ if the housemates like the song or ☹ if they don't like it.

Song	Zac	Gaby	Neena	Me
The river				
Move				
Chimes				
Check it out				

C **SPEAK** What do you think of the songs? Complete the *Me* column of the table with ☺ or ☹.

FUNCTIONAL LANGUAGE

Asking for and giving opinions

A Complete the table with the phrases in the box.

I hate it. I like it. I love it! I really hate it. It's good. I think it's awful. I'm not sure. It's awesome! It's great! It isn't great.

Asking for opinions	What do you think of it/this? How about you?
Giving opinions	😊😊😊 ______ 😊😊 ______ ______ 😊 ______ ______ ☹ ______ ______ ☹☹ ______ ☹☹☹ ______

B Rank the adjectives below from 😊😊😊 (very positive) to ☹☹☹ (very negative). Then, compare your answers with a partner.

1 great ☺☺
2 amazing ______
3 bad ______
4 awful ______
5 happy ______
6 sad ______
7 terrible ______
8 good ______

MILLY

SAM

NEENA

ZAC

GABY

USEFUL PHRASES

A Match the beginnings (1–7) and the endings (a–g) of the useful phrases.

1	That's	a	sorry.	___
2	OK	b	one then.	___
3	I'm	c	it?	___
4	It makes me	d	go!	___
5	OK. Not that	e	Let's add it to the playlist.	___
6	My	f	then.	___
7	Finally!	g	feel sad.	___

B Watch the video again. Check your answers to Exercise A. Who says it? Write G (Gaby), N (Neena) or Z (Zac) next to each useful phrase.

PRONUNCIATION

Stress and intonation

6.8 **A** Listen and repeat. Copy the stress and intonation.

B Work in pairs. Student A – name a song, a singer or a band. Student B – give your opinion. Take turns.

A: Ed Sheeran.
B: He's OK. How about Haim?
A: I love them!

SPEAKING

A PREPARE Imagine you are going on a road trip. Make a list of your five favorite songs.

B SPEAK Work in small groups. Agree on a playlist of ten songs for your road trip. Use phrases from the Functional language section to help you.

C PRESENT Work in pairs. Compare your playlist. Do you like the same music?

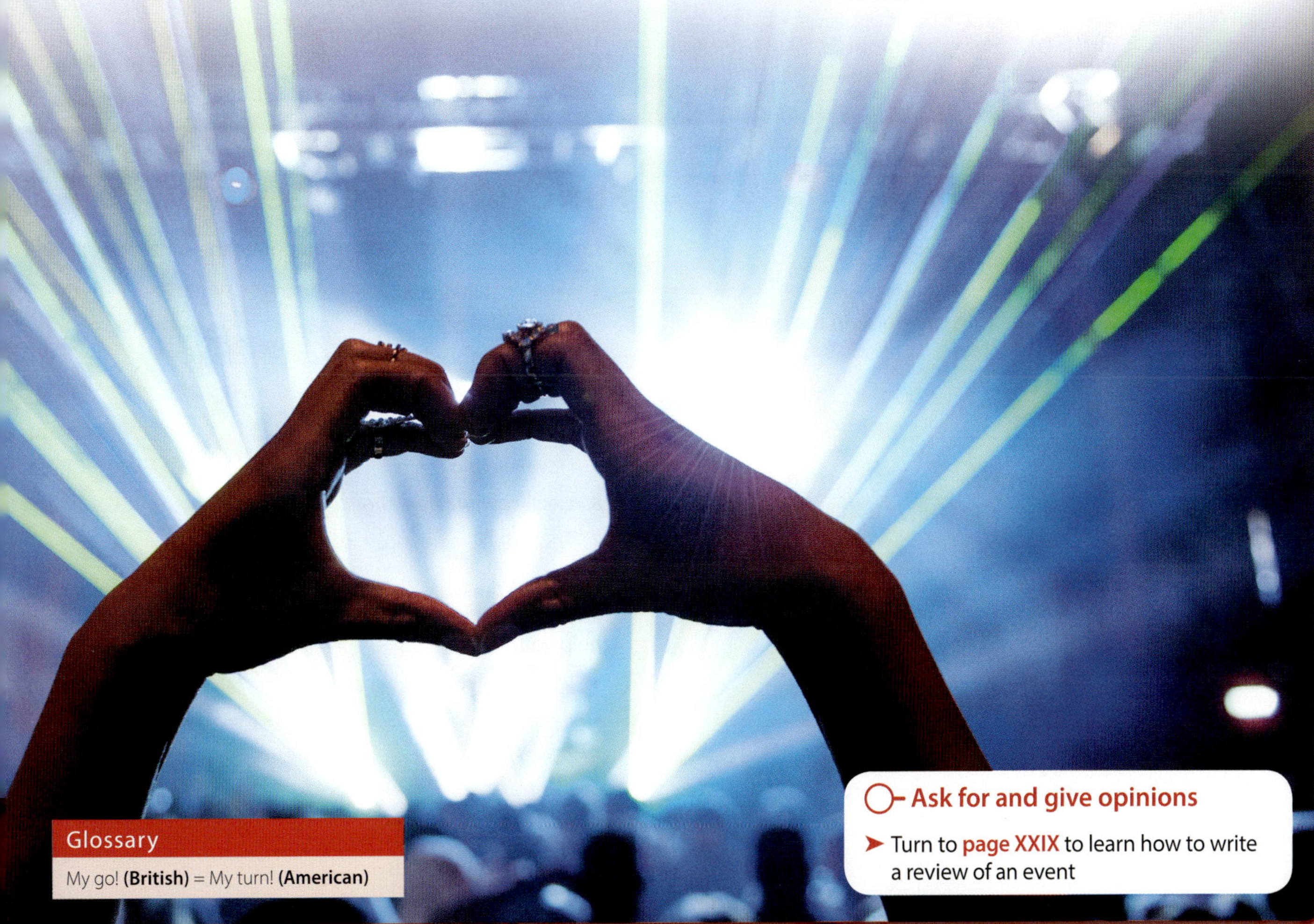

Glossary

My go! **(British)** = My turn! **(American)**

Ask for and give opinions

➤ Turn to **page XXIX** to learn how to write a review of an event

GRAMMAR

A Write sentences about what Kyle likes and dislikes.

♥ love — ☺ like — ☹ don't like — 😣 hate

1 play soccer ♥ *Kyle loves playing soccer.*
2 dance ☹ ________
3 go clothes shopping 😣 ________
4 Wes Anderson movies ☺ ________
5 watch basketball ☺ ________
6 listen to jazz music 😣 ________
7 play video games ♥ ________
8 Japanese food ☹ ________

B Complete the conversation with *was*, *were*, *wasn't* or *weren't*.

A: [1] *Were* you at home last night?
B: No, I [2]________. I [3]________ at a comedy show.
A: Where [4]________ your roommates?
B: They [5]________ out, too.
A: [6]________ they at the concert?
B: No, they [7]________.

C Complete the text with the simple past form of the verbs in parentheses.

In 2016, Elvis Presley [1] *was* (*be*) on the Forbes list of highest-paid dead entertainers. He [2]________ (*earn*) $27 million! Other musicians on the list [3]________ (*include*) Prince and David Bowie, who both [4]________ (*die*) in 2016. David Bowie [5]________ (*make*) his last album *Blackstar* in 2016. He [6]________ (*get*) $10.5 million. Prince [7]________ (*sell*) more than 2.5 million albums last year.

VOCABULARY

A Complete the conversation with the words in the box.

concert exhibit festival movie play

Luis: Do you like Picasso? There's an [1]________ of his paintings.
Manu: I don't like looking at paintings.
Luis: OK. Well, how about going to see a [2]________ at the movie theater.
Manu: Hmm. I'm not sure.
Luis: There's a [3]________ at the theater.
Manu: That's boring. I want to listen to some music. There's a rock [4]________ on tonight.
Luis: But I hate rock music.
Manu: Oh, right. There's a jazz music [5]________ this weekend. It's in the park. It starts at 2 pm.

B Complete the sentences with *in*, *last*, *ago* and *yesterday*.

1 I went to my first concert *in* 2010.
2 We saw that band two weeks ________.
3 The exhibit opened ________.
4 I met my best friend ________ year.
5 The first 3D movies were ________ the 1920s.
6 I went to the movie theater ________ afternoon.

C Complete the sentences with the verbs in the box.

became got had moved started studied was went

1 My grandmother ________ born in 1959.
2 I ________ an English teacher in 2015.
3 My parents ________ married on a beach in Hawaii.
4 My brother ________ to Oxford University to study law.
5 Sarah ________ a baby a few months ago.
6 My sister ________ to a new house last summer.
7 Beth ________ her new job two days ago.
8 I ________ history in college.

D SPEAK Work in pairs. Tell your partner about five important events in your life.

A: A really important event in my life was getting married. I got married in 2016. It was sunny. I was very happy. What about you?
B: That sounds amazing! An important event in my life was starting college. I met lots of interesting people on my first day.

FUNCTIONAL LANGUAGE

A Choose the correct words to complete the sentences.

1 What do you ***think*** / ***know*** about the singer Katy Perry? I think she's great.
2 Listen to this! I ***think*** / ***sure*** Foals are great.
3 How ***about*** / ***think*** you?
4 I'm not ***sure*** / ***know*** about that.
5 I ***love*** / ***loving*** them!
6 I really ***awful*** / ***hate*** them!
7 This exhibit is boring. It isn't ***great*** / ***sure***.

B SPEAK Work in pairs. Take turns asking and answering about these things. Use the sentences in Exercise A to help you.

- a band you like / don't like
- a famous singer
- a popular movie
- a movie you like

A: I love the new Jennifer Lawrence movie.
B: Me too! She's a great actress.

Endmatter Contents

Grammar Hub

Vocabulary Hub

Communication Hub

Writing

Grammar Hub

1.1 Simple present *be*: positive and negative

	Positive	Negative
I	**I am** in this class. **I'm** in this class.	**I am not** in this class. **I'm not** in this class.
he/she/it	**She is** South Korean. **She's** South Korean.	**He is not** South Korean. **He isn't** South Korean.
you/we/they	**They are** from Japan. **They're** from Japan.	**We are not** from Japan. **We aren't** from Japan.

- We use *be* to talk about states, facts and personal details, e.g. name, nationality, age or status.
- We use a noun or subject pronoun (*I*, *you*, etc) before the verb *be*.

He's South Korean. NOT ~~Is South Korean.~~

- We often use contractions when we speak.

*I **am** 20 years old. → I**'m** 20 years old.*

- In the negative contraction, we can also say: *You're not*, *He's not*, *She's not*, etc.

*She **isn't** 24 years old. OR She**'s not** 24 years old.*

Be careful!

- We use *you* for one person and more than one person.

*Tony, **you're** in this class.*
*Tony and Paola, **you're** in this class.*

1.2 Simple present *be*: questions

Question	Positive short answer	Negative short answer
Am I in this class?	Yes, **you are**.	No, **you aren't**.
Are you married?	Yes, **I am**.	No, **I'm not**.
Is he/she/it French?	Yes, **he/she/it is**.	No, **he/she/it isn't**.
Are we in this class?	Yes, **you/we are**.	No, **you/we aren't**.
Are you married?	Yes, **we are**.	No, **we aren't**.
Are they friends?	Yes, **they are**.	No, **they aren't**.

- In questions, the subject pronoun (*I*, *you*, *he*, *she*) comes after the verb *be*.

Am I in this class? NOT ~~I am in this class?~~

- In negative short answers we can also say: *No, you're not.*, *No, he's not.*, *No, she's not.*, etc.

Be careful!

- In positive short answers, we don't use contractions.

Yes, she is. NOT ~~Yes, she's.~~

Question word + *be* + subject + ?	
Age	**How old are** you?
Place	**Where are** you from?
Thing	**What's** your name?

1.3 *a/an* and plural nouns; *this, that, these, those*

- We use *a/an* with singular nouns.
- We use *a* with nouns that begin with a consonant sound (e.g. *s*, *w*) and *an* with nouns with a vowel sound (*a*, *e*, *i*, *o*, *u*).

a	**a s**andwich **a w**allet
an	**an e**mail **an a**irport

- We don't use *a* or *an* with plural nouns.

	Singular	Plural
Add **-s**.	pen	pen**s**
Add **-es** to nouns that end **-s** or **-ch**.	addre**ss** wat**ch**	address**es** watch**es**
Change **-y** after a consonant to **-ies**.	countr**y** nationalit**y**	countr**ies** nationalit**ies**
Some nouns are irregular.	man child person	men children people

	this	With a singular noun that's near	**This** is my bag here.
	that	With a singular noun that's far	**That** is Paola's bag over there.
	these	With a plural noun that's near	**These** are our bags here.
	those	With a plural noun that's far	**Those** are your bags over there.

- In questions, the verb *be* comes before *this*, *that*, *these* or *those*.

***Is that** your bag over there? NOT ~~That is your bag over there?~~*

1.1 Simple present *be*: positive and negative

A Choose the correct form of *be* for each subject.

1 I *am / is / are*
2 you *am / is / are*
3 it *am / is / are*
4 they *am / is / are*
5 she *am / is / are*
6 we *am / is / are*

B Choose the correct form of *be* for each subject.

1 I ___am___ Italian.
2 We ________ married.
3 She ________ my friend.
4 It ________ 20 years old.
5 You ________ in class 4A.
6 Asim and Akil ________ Egyptian.

C Rewrite the sentences in the positive and negative. Use contractions.

	POSITIVE (+)	NEGATIVE (-)
1 He is sorry.	He's sorry.	He isn't sorry.
2 They are friends.	________	________
3 We are from Turkey.	________	________
4 You are famous!	________	________
5 It is Spanish.	________	________
6 She is in this class.	________	________

➤ Go back to page 3.

1.2 Simple present *be*: questions

A Use the prompts to write questions and short answers.

1 you / married
___Are you married___ (?) ___No, I'm not.___ (-)
2 your hometown / nice
________________ (?) ________________ (+)
3 they / your new shoes
________________ (?) ________________ (+)
4 he / in a relationship
________________ (?) ________________ (-)
5 you / Turkish
________________ (?) ________________ (-)
6 you / a student
________________ (?) ________________ (+)

B Write *be* in the simple present in each blank.

1 What ___is___ your favorite food?
2 Where ________ you from?
3 How old ________ you?
4 What ________ your flight number?
5 Where ________ Max from?
6 How old ________ Cara?

➤ Go back to page 5.

1.3 *a*/*an* and plural nouns; *this, that, these, those*

A Complete the sentences with *a* or *an*.

1 MSU is ___a___ university in Moscow.
2 Take ________ umbrella – it's raining!
3 Tonya is ________ French student.
4 Send me ________ email later.
5 Mexico is ________ country in South America.
6 This is ________ example.

B Complete the sentences with the plural form of the nouns in bold.

1 Are these your ___keys___? **key**
2 There are two ________________ for you. **sandwich**
3 Where are my ________________? **headphone**
4 Harvard and Stanford are ________________ in the US. **university**
5 He has six different ________________! **watch**
6 Poland and Sweden are ________________ in Europe. **country**

C Look at pictures (1–6) and choose the correct words to complete the sentences.

1 Is *this / that / those* your wallet?

2 *Those / These / This* are my sunglasses.

3 *This / Those / These* are my sandwiches.

4 Are *these / those / that* bags yours?

5 *This / These / Those* suitcase is really heavy!

6 Is *those / that / this* your pen?

➤ Go back to page 7.

Grammar Hub

2.1 Possessive adjectives and apostrophes

Subject pronouns	Possessive adjectives
I	my
he	his
she	her
it	its
we	our
you	your
they	their

Be careful!

- We only add *'s* to the last name.

  Ivan and Hannah's family NOT ~~Ivan's and Hannah's family~~
- We don't put an apostrophe in *its* when it is a possessive adjective.

  *France is famous for **its** cheese. NOT ~~France is famous for it's cheese.~~*
- We only add 's to last name when the thing referred to belongs to both people. If you are talking about two different things (Ivan's blog and Hannah's blog - We read Ivan's and Hannah's blogs) both would get the apostrophe.

- We use possessive adjectives to show that something belongs to someone.

  *Ali lives with **her** parents.*

  *I live with Tom and **his** sister.*
- We use the same possessive adjectives for singular and plural nouns.

  *They're **her** friends. NOT ~~They're hers friends.~~*
- We use possessive apostrophes to show that something belongs to someone.

  She's married to Dave's brother.
- We use *'s* with singular nouns.

  My sister's children are named Tanya and Kyle.
- We use *s'* with plural nouns.

  My grandparents' names are Ed and Jilly.
- We use *'s* with irregular plural nouns.

  The children's names are Moya and Daryl.

2.2 *have/has*

	Positive	Negative
I/you/we/they	**I have** a roommate.	**I don't have** a roommate.
he/she/it	**He has** a big family.	**She doesn't have** a big family.

- We use *have/has* to talk about someone's appearance, family or possessions.

  I have a new phone.
- We use *Have/Has* + subject to make questions.
- We often use *any* before plural nouns in the question form.

  *Does she have **any** children?*

	Question	Short answers	
I/you/we/they	**Do you have** any brothers or sisters?	Yes, **I do**.	No, **I don't**.
he/she/it	**Does she have** long hair?	Yes, **she does.**	No, **she doesn't.**

Be careful!

Does she have any children? Yes, she does. NOT ~~Yes, she has.~~

2.3 Using adjectives

- We use adjectives to describe things.
- Adjectives have one form for singular and plural.

  a kind woman

  two kind women NOT ~~two kinds women~~
- In sentences with a noun, the adjective comes before the noun.

  *She is a **good** friend.*
- The adjective comes after the verb *be* when we describe the subject of a sentence.

  *Frederica **is tall**.*

Be careful!

- We use *very* and *really* to make an adjective stronger.

  ***very** tall*
- We use *fairly* to mean 'a little but not very'.

  ***fairly** long*
- *Very*, *really* and *fairly* come before the adjective.

  *Her hair is **very/really/fairly** long.*

2.1 Possessive adjectives and apostrophes

A Complete the sentences with a possessive adjective.

1 My cousin and his wife live in Paris. ________ house is very big.
2 Sofia Coppola is a screenwriter and director. ________ movies are famous.
3 Switzerland is famous for ________ chocolate.
4 We're French, but ________ children speak English at home.
5 Ken, is ________ last name 'Clark' or 'Clerk'?
6 That's Michael with ________ wife, Laura.
7 I'm British, but ________ parents are German.

B Choose the correct options to complete the sentences.

1 My ***husband's / husbands'*** family lives in Brazil.
2 Their ***daughter's / daughters'*** name is Lillie.
3 The ***children's / childrens'*** grandfather is an artist.
4 My ***grandparent's / grandparents'*** names are Mel and Bob.
5 What are the ***women's / womens'*** names?

C Choose the correct words to complete the text.

[1]***I / My*** am an actor, and so is my father. [2]***He / His*** name is Juan. [3]***He's / His*** famous in South America. [4]***I / My*** mother is famous too. [5]***She's / Her*** a singer. I also have two brothers. [6]***Their / They*** names are Miguel and Esteban. [7]***Their / They're*** singers like [8]***we / our*** mother.

➤ Go back to page 13.

2.2 *have/has*

A Complete the sentences using *have* or *has*.

1 They ________ a house in the countryside.
2 Georgiana and Stefania ________ long, blond hair.
3 Diane ________ a twin sister named Erin.
4 My sister ________ brown eyes, but I don't.
5 They ________ three children.

B Rewrite the sentences in Exercise A to make them negative. Use contractions where possible.

1 *They don't have a house in the countryside.*
2 ________
3 ________
4 ________
5 ________

C Use the prompts to write questions and short answers.

1 your dad / a beard
Does your dad have a beard? (?) *No, he doesn't.* (-)
2 you / any lipstick
________ (?) ________ (+)
3 they / a car
________ (?) ________ (+)
4 Maria / short hair
________ (?) ________ (+)
5 we / any shampoo
________ (?) ________ (+)
6 you / your glasses
________ (?) ________ (-)

➤ Go back to page 15.

2.3 Using adjectives

A Reorder the words to make sentences.

1 busy / is / it / here / in
____
2 happy / today / Tim / is
____
3 is / Al's / desk / really / messy
____
4 house / really / is / big / this
____
5 a / has / he / car / fast
____
6 really / sister's / funny / your
____

B Correct the mistakes in each sentence.

1 Toby is ~~a~~ fairly noisy.
2 Roxanna is a really friendly.
3 Marin is a big very man.
4 Greg is serious really.
5 Magdalena has a very bedroom messy.
6 Alicia and Georgina are quiets young women.
7 Wow! These paintings are beautifuls.
8 This café is quiet fairly.

➤ Go back to page 16.

Grammar Hub

3.1 Simple present positive

I/you/we/they	**I finish** work at 5 pm.
he/she/it	**She finishes** work at 5 pm.

- We use the simple present to talk about habits and routines.
- We also use the simple present to talk about:
  - facts and things that are true.

    Paris is the capital of France.
  - likes and dislikes.

    Alessia likes her apartment.
  - possessions with *have* and *has*.

    He has a pet dog.
  - fixed times.

    The movie starts at 6 pm.

Spelling rules		
Add **-s** to most verbs.	love play	She love**s** music. He play**s** computer games.
Add **-es** to verbs that end **-ss, -ch, -sh, -x, -o.**	wat**ch** g**o**	She watch**es** TV. He go**es** for a run.
Change **-y** after a consonant to **-ies.**	stud**y**	She stud**ies** after dinner.

Be careful!

- The *he/she/it* form of *have* is *has*.

  She has a nice flat. NOT ~~*She haves a nice flat.*~~

3.2 Adverbs of frequency

0% ← → 100%

never — rarely — sometimes — often — usually — always

- We use adverbs of frequency to talk about how regularly we do things.
- Adverbs of frequency go after *be* and *can*.

  *It's **usually** busy on a Saturday.*

  *I **can never** find my keys in the morning.*
- Adverbs of frequency go before other verbs.

  *I **sometimes play** soccer on Saturdays.*
- Look at where the adverbs go in questions.

  ***How often do** you play soccer?*

  *What time **do you usually eat** dinner?*

3.3 Simple present negative

	do/does not + base form
I/you/we/they	**I don't cook** every evening.
he/she/it	**She doesn't cook** every evening.

Be careful!

With *he/she/it* forms, we don't add -*s* to the verb.

It doesn't start at 8 o'clock. NOT ~~*It doesn't starts at 8 o'clock.*~~

- We use the simple present negative to talk about habits and routines.

  I do not exercise on the weekend.
- We also use the simple present negative to talk about:
  - facts and things that are true.

    I don't live in London.
  - dislikes.

    Sarah doesn't like sushi.
  - possessions with *have* and *has*.

    They don't have any children.
  - fixed times.

    The store doesn't open until 6 pm.
- We use the contraction *don't* (*do not*) and *doesn't* (*does not*).

3.1 Simple present positive

A Complete the sentences with the correct form of the verb in parentheses.

1 I ________________ (live) in an apartment in Hong Kong.
2 My mother ________________ (watch) TV every day.
3 We ________________ (listen) to the same music.
4 She ________________ (have) a gym class after work.
5 My dad ________________ (go) to work by train.
6 The store ________________ (close) at ten o'clock.

B Rewrite the sentences. Correct the mistakes in bold.

1 They **works** in an office. ________________
2 She **study** every day. ________________
3 He **gos** to school at eight o'clock. ________________
4 I **buys** sandwiches for lunch every day. ________________
5 Our dog **watch** TV with us. ________________
6 We **eats** dinner at seven o'clock. ________________
7 She **live** in New York with her sister. ________________
8 The train **leave** at 10:30 am. ________________

➤ Go back to page 23.

3.2 Adverbs of frequency

A Reorder the words to make sentences.

1 by train / go to work / I / never
I never go to work by train.
2 play / we / video games / often
____
3 always / the radio / they / in the car / listen to
____
4 home / he / rarely / before seven / is
____
5 busy / is / usually / Andrea / on the weekend / ?
____
6 work late / you / do / sometimes / ?
____

B Rewrite the sentences using the adverbs in parentheses.

1 I go to the gym. (never)
I never go to the gym.
2 I read in bed. (often)
____
3 Eleni plays soccer on Sundays. (usually)
____
4 Dan's late for his English class. (sometimes)
____
5 I eat sushi. (rarely)
____
6 Lin goes to bed at 11 pm. (always)
____

➤ Go back to page 24.

3.3 Simple present negative

A Complete the sentences with the correct form of the verb in parentheses.

1 He *doesn't have* (not have) coffee with breakfast.
2 I ________________ (not like) jazz music.
3 You ________________ (not need) a coat – it's really hot outside!
4 We ________________ (not have) children.
5 Amy ________________ (not go) to the movie theater very often.
6 Zach ________________ (not work) in an office.
7 My parents ________________ (not work) anymore. They're retired.

B Rewrite the sentences in the negative.

1 Sam likes parties.
Sam doesn't like parties.
2 We usually have lunch in the kitchen.
____
3 Eleni speaks Arabic.
____
4 They have a big house.
____
5 I listen to music on the train.
____
6 Lin watches TV in the morning.
____

➤ Go back to page 26.

Grammar Hub

4.1 Simple present *yes/no* questions; short answers

	Question	Short answers	
I/you/we/they	**Do I have** a meeting today?	Yes, **you do**.	No, **you don't**.
he/she/it	**Does it have** a good camera?	Yes, **it does**.	No, **it doesn't**.

- We use simple present *yes/no* questions to ask about habits and routines.
- We use *Do/Does* + subject + base form to make questions.

Be careful!

Does she like tea? NOT ~~*Does she likes tea?*~~
Yes, she does. NOT ~~*Yes, she likes.*~~

4.2 *have to / don't have to*

	Positive	Negative
I/you/we/they	**I have to work** on the weekend.	**I don't have to work** on the weekend.
he/she/it	**She has to wear** a uniform.	She **doesn't have to wear** a uniform.

	Question	Short answers	
I/you/we/they	**Do I have to** start at 9 am?	Yes, **you do**.	No, **you don't**.
he/she/it	**Does she have to** travel a lot for work?	Yes, **she does**.	No, **she doesn't**.

- We use *have to* + base form without *to* to talk about rules and things we need to do.
- We use *don't/doesn't have to* to talk about things we don't need to do.
- We use *Do/Does* + subject + *have to* + base form to make questions.

Be careful!

I don't have to work long hours. NOT ~~*I haven't to work long hours.*~~
Do I have to work long hours? NOT ~~*Have I to work long hours?*~~
No, you don't. NOT ~~*No, you haven't.*~~

4.3 Question words

Why	To ask for a reason	**Why** are you late?
What	To ask about a thing	**What** does it do?
Where	To ask about a place	**Where** do you work?
Who	To ask about a person	**Who** is your boss?
How much	To ask about a quantity	**How much** does it cost?
How long	To ask about a length of time	**How long** does the movie last?
When	To ask about a time	**When** does the meeting start?

- We use question word + auxiliary verb + subject + main verb to make *Wh-* questions.

Where do you live? NOT ~~*Where you live?*~~
How much does it cost? NOT ~~*How much it costs?*~~

4.1 Simple present *yes/no* questions; short answers

A Complete the questions with *Do* or *Does*.

1 ___Do___ you work in an office?
2 ________ they work from home?
3 ________ she work with animals?
4 ________ he like his job?
5 ________ we wear a uniform?
6 ________ it have a name?
7 ________ it get busy on the weekend?
8 ________ your sisters work in London?

B Use the prompts to write questions and short answers.

1 you / work / part time
___Do you work part time?___ (?) ___Yes, I do.___ (+)
2 they / live / in the city center
________________ (?) ________________ (-)
3 she / wear / a uniform
________________ (?) ________________ (+)
4 he / travel / for his job
________________ (?) ________________ (-)
5 you / speak / French
________________ (?) ________________ (+)

➤ Go back to page 33.

4.2 *have to / don't have to*

A Choose the correct options to complete the sentences.

1 You ***has to / have to*** take your shoes off first.
2 You ***haven't to / don't have to*** wear a uniform.
3 She ***don't / doesn't*** have to pay the hotel bill.
4 ***You do / Do you*** have to get up early?
5 ***Has he to / Does he have to*** work nine to five?
6 A: Do I have to pay for training?
B: Yes, you ***don't / do.***

B Complete the sentences with the correct form of *have to*.

1 Doctors ________ work long hours.
2 I ________ go to bed early. It's a weekend.
3 He ________ wear a tie. He's a chef.
4 You ________ study hard to learn a language.
5 Sally ________ study. She has an exam tomorrow.

C Complete the conversations with the correct form of *have to* and short answers.

1 A: ___Do you have to pay___ (you / pay) for food at work?
B: Yes, ___I do___.
2 A: ________________ (I / wear) a uniform?
B: Yes, ________________.
3 A: ________________ (she / finish) it today?
B: No, ________________.
4 A: ________________ (they / take) a course?
B: Yes, ________________.
5 A: ________________ (he study) tonight?
B: Yes, ________________.
6 A: ________________ (we pay) for training?
B: No, ________________.

➤ Go back to page 34.

4.3 Question words

A Complete the sentences with the question words in the box.

how what when where who why

1 ________________ do most college students live?
2 ________________ is your teacher?
3 ________________ long is the course?
4 ________________ class do you have now?
5 ________________ do you want to work there?
6 ________________ does your course start?

B Reorder the words to make questions.

1 do / where / you / study
___Where do you study?___
2 much / it / how / does / cost
____
3 long / last / how / it / does
____
4 the / when / course / does / start
____
5 course / study / what / you / do
____

➤ Go back to page 36.

Grammar Hub

5.1 *there is/are*

	Positive	Negative
Singular	**There's** a dishwasher in the kitchen.	**There isn't** a TV in the living room.
Plural	**There are** four chairs in the dining room.	**There aren't** any cushions on the couch.

	Question	Short answers	
Singular	**Is there** a microwave in the kitchen?	Yes, **there is**.	No, **there isn't**.
Plural	**Are there** any tomatoes in the fridge?	Yes, **there are**.	No, **there aren't**.

- We use *there is / there are* to say that something exists and talk about position.

  There's a coffee machine in the kitchen.

  There are more plates in the cupboard.
- We use *any* in negative sentences and questions with plural nouns and uncountable nouns.

  *There aren't **any** plates in the cupboard.*

  *Is there **any** milk in the fridge?*

Be careful!

- In a list of nouns, we use *there is* when the first is singular.

  There is a coffee maker, two cups and three plates on the table.
- In a list of nouns, we use *there are* when the first is plural.

  There are two cups, three plates and a coffee maker on the table.

5.2 *can*

	Positive	Negative
I/you/he/she/it/we/they	She **can swim**.	She **can't swim**.

- We use *can* to talk about ability and what is possible.
- In the negative, we can also say *cannot*.

  *She **can't** swim. OR She **cannot** swim.*

	Question	Short answers	
I/you/he/she/it/we/they	**Can we go** to the movie theater?	Yes, you **can**.	No, you **can't**.

Be careful!

He can sing. NOT ~~He cans sing.~~ NOT ~~He can to sing.~~

5.3 Imperatives

- We use imperatives to tell someone to do something.

  Call me later.

  Look at this website.

  Give me your phone.

  Open your books to page 23.
- We can use *please* to make imperatives more polite.

  Please ask at the front desk.
- We use *don't* to tell someone not to do something.

  Don't walk in the park at night.

Be careful!

Give me your phone. NOT ~~To give me your phone.~~

5.1 *there is/are*

A Complete the sentences with *is* or *are*.

1 ______________ there a microwave in the kitchen?
2 There ______________ a mirror in the bathroom.
3 There ______________ some eggs in the fridge.
4 There ______________ some people here to see you.
5 ______________ there any bedrooms upstairs?
6 ______________ there a coffee machine?

B Use the prompts to write questions and short answers.

1 plates / in the cupboard
Are there any plates in the cupboard? (?) *No, there aren't.* (-)
2 dishwasher / in the kitchen
______________ (?) ______________ (+)
3 swimming pool / in the yard
______________ (?) ______________ (-)
4 tomatoes / in the fridge
______________ (?) ______________ (-)
5 TV / in the bedroom
______________ (?) ______________ (-)
6 socks / in that drawer
______________ (?) ______________ (+)

➤ Go back to page 43.

5.2 *can*

A Complete the sentences with *can* or *can't*.

1 I'm sorry. I ______________ come on Saturday, I have to work.
2 ______________ you open the window, please? It's very hot in here.
3 She's not here I'm afraid. ______________ I take a message?
4 She ______________ come out tonight, because she doesn't have any money.
5 I ______________ speak Japanese, but not write it.
6 We ______________ buy it now. The store is closed.

B Use the prompts to write sentences with *can*.

1 I / play / the guitar
____
2 they / leave / work / whenever they want
____
3 she / speak / Arabic / ?
____
4 where / I / buy / laundry detergent / ?
____
5 I / stay / at your house / tonight / ?
____

➤ Go back to page 45.

5.3 Imperatives

A Complete the sentences with the verbs in the box.

close drink drive play talk read sit

1 Don't ______________ soccer on the grass.
2 ______________ the door behind you.
3 ______________ on the right.
4 Don't ______________ in the library.
5 Don't ______________ the water.
6 ______________ this – it's really interesting!
7 Please ______________ down!

B Match the verbs (1–6) with the phrases (a–f) to make imperative sentences.

1 Go	a me more about amazing buildings.
2 Tell	b the window. It's hot.
3 Learn	c the rooftop gardens.
4 Look at	d your shoes off, please.
5 Open	e some Portuguese words before you go.
6 Take	f away.

➤ Go back to page 47.

Grammar Hub

6.1 Likes and dislikes

	verb + *-ing*	verb + noun
☺☺	I **love going** to concerts. She **loves going** to concerts.	I **love photography**. He **loves photography**.
☺	I **like watching** TV. He **likes watching** TV.	I **like rock music**. She **likes rock music**.
☹	I **don't like visiting** exhibits. She **doesn't like visiting** exhibits.	I **don't like pizza**. He **doesn't like pizza**.
☹☹	I **hate doing** the dishes. She **hates doing** the dishes.	I **hate cold weather**. He **hates cold weather**.

6.2 *was/were*

	Positive	Negative
I/he/she/it	**I was** at the theater.	**I was not** at the theater. **I wasn't** at the theater.
you/we/they	**They were** at the movie theater.	**They were not** at the movie theater. **They weren't** at the movie theater.

- We use *was/were* to talk about things that happened in the past.
- We often use these time expressions with *was/were*.

I was there two hours ***ago****.*
They were here ***last night****.*
It was my birthday ***on Sunday****.*
I was busy ***on the weekend****.*
We were out ***yesterday****.*

	Question	Short answers	
I/he/she/it	**Was it** interesting?	Yes, **it was**.	No, **it wasn't**.
you/we/they	**Were they** out last night?	Yes, **they were**.	No, **they weren't**.

6.3 Simple past regular and irregular verbs

Regular verbs		
Base form	**Simple past**	
ask	ask**ed**	**I asked** for help.
like	like**d**	**She liked** the comedy show.
stop	stopp**ed**	**You stopped** the car.
study	stud**ied**	**We studied** English last night.
Irregular verbs		
Base form	**Simple past**	
become	became	**He became** a singer.
go	went	**They went** shopping.
have	had	**We had** very little money.
send	sent	**They sent** you an email.
write	wrote	**I wrote** you a letter.
win	won	**She won** the game.

Spelling rules	Base form	Simple past
Add **-ed**.	join	join**ed**
Add **-d** to verbs ending **-e**.	lik**e**	like**d**
Change **-y** after a consonant to **-ied**.	stud**y**	stud**ied**
Double the consonant and add **-ed** with verbs ending in vowel + consonant.	st**op**	sto**pped**

6.1 Likes and dislikes

A Complete the sentences with the words in the box.

doesn't going like loves singing

1 My dad ________________ Elvis. He has all his albums.
2 I like ________________ in the shower.
3 She ________________ like horror movies. She gets scared.
4 You don't ________________ cheese, do you?
5 Bill hates ________________ to art galleries.

B Correct the mistakes in each sentence.

1 She likes ~~to~~ rock music.
2 I don't liking photography.
3 They love stay in on Friday nights.
4 We love to sitting outside.
5 How can you hating the *Star Wars* movies?
6 He not like sushi.

C Use the prompts to write sentences with *love, like, don't like* and *hate*.

1 Sheila / ☺☺ / go to the theater.
Sheila loves going to the theater.
2 Owen / ☹ / visit / his grandparents.
____
3 We / ☺ / watch / *Game of Thrones*.
____
4 I / ☹☹ / clean / the bathroom.
____
5 I / ☺☺ / dance.
____
6 They / ☹ / clean / their bedroom.
____

➤ Go back to page 53.

6.2 *was/were*

A Complete the sentences with *was* or *were*.

1 Wow! That show ____________ amazing!
2 TVs ____________ really expensive in the 1950s.
3 ____________ Yuki there on Saturday?
4 There ____________ a lot of people at the party.
5 Where ____________ you last night?
6 The tickets ____________ really expensive.

B Complete the text messages with *was, were, wasn't* and *weren't*.

Hi Malc! I __*was*__ at an exhibit on Saturday. My friends Roma and Pete [1]____________ there, too. There [2]____________ any good paintings – we hated them all! How [3]____________ your weekend?

Hal and I were at a comedy show. It was fun! [4]____________ you out on Sunday?

Yeah. We [5]____________ at the big soccer game. And you?

I was at home studying. [6]____________ the soccer game good?

It was great.

➤ Go back to page 54.

6.3 Simple past regular and irregular verbs

A Complete the sentences with the simple past form of the verbs in the box.

ask like play stay stop study

1 I can't believe I failed. I ____________ all night for that test!
2 I really ____________ Michael Jackson when I was younger.
3 They ____________ work to have lunch.
4 I think he ____________ for the university rugby team.
5 She ____________ Rob to come, but he was busy.
6 We ____________ at home and watched *The Walking Dead* last night.

B Complete the sentences in the simple past with the verbs in parentheses.

1 David Bowie ____________ (die) in 2016.
2 John Lennon ____________ (leave) the Beatles in 1970.
3 Chris Brown ____________ (write) the hit song 'Disturbia'.
4 The movie *La La Land* ____________ (win) six Academy Awards.
5 Before he was an actor, Sylvester Stallone ____________ (teach) gymnastics.
6 Bob Dylan ____________ (take) his stage name from the poet Dylan Thomas.

C Correct the mistakes in each sentence.

1 Real Madrid ~~winned~~ *won* the game 2–0.
2 He teached history for twenty years.
3 She writed nine books in her lifetime.
4 We taked a taxi to the restaurant.
5 She leaved work early last night.
6 You sended the letter two weeks ago!

➤ Go back to page 57.

Vocabulary Hub

1.1 Countries and nationalities

A Match countries (1–12) with the words in the box.

Brazil Chile China Egypt France
India Italy Japan Portugal
Spain Thailand Turkey

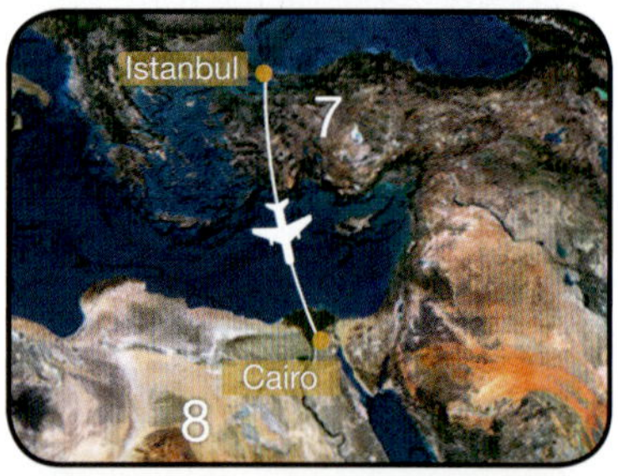

1 ________ 7 ________
2 ________ 8 ________
3 ________ 9 ________
4 ________ 10 ________
5 ________ 11 ________
6 ________ 12 ________

B Complete the table with the words in the box.

British Greek Russia Poland ~~South Korean~~
Swedish Switzerland Vietnamese

Country	Nationality
	-ian/-an
Colombia	Colombian
South Korea	1 South Korean
2 ________	Russian
	-ish
Finland	Finnish
3 ________	Polish
Sweden	4 ________
	-ese
Sudan	Sudanese
Vietnam	5 ________
	Other
The Netherlands	Dutch
Greece	6 ________
7 ________	Swiss
the UK	8 ________

➤ Go back to page 2

2.2 Describing appearance

A Complete the table with the words in the box.

bald a beard glasses large
a mustache short slim tall

Face / head:	
Height:	
Build:	

B Match the descriptions (1–5) with the pictures (a–e).

a

c

e

b

d

1 She's tall and has curly hair. ___
2 She has long, straight hair and glasses. ___
3 He has red hair and a mustache. ___
4 He has light hair and blue eyes. ___
5 He's short and bald. ___

➤ Go back to page 14

3.1 Everyday activities

Match photos (1–9) with the activities.

___ listen to music ___ watch TV ___ take a shower ___ go to the movie theater ___ go for a run
___ have coffee with friends ___ go to bed ___ read a book ___ have lunch

➤ Go back to page 22

4.1 Work and jobs

Match the photos (1–8) with the words in the box.

___ dentist ___ designer ___ hairdresser ___ journalist ___ mechanic ___ nurse ___ police officer ___ sales clerk

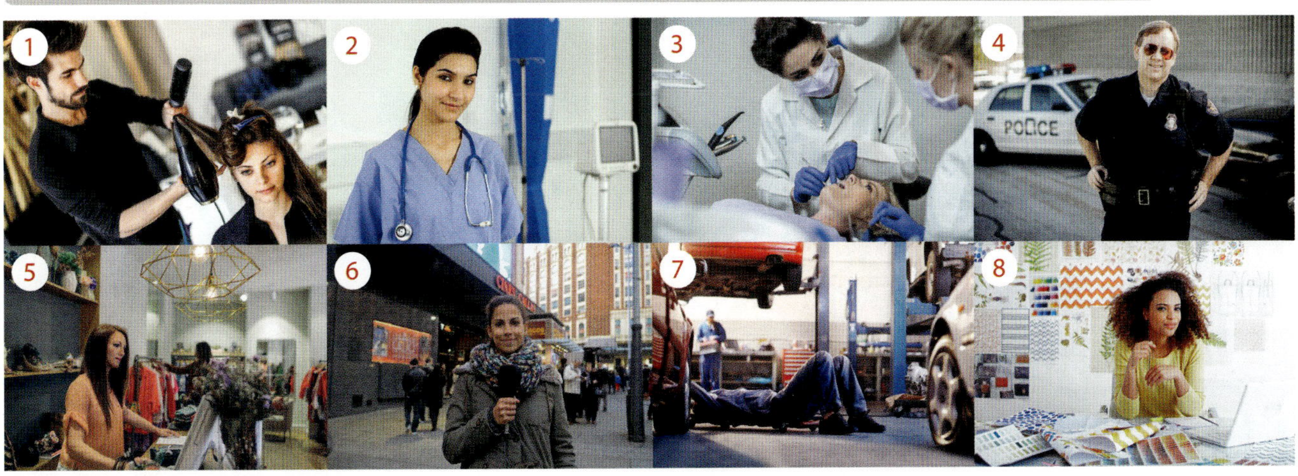

➤ Go back to page 32

Vocabulary Hub

5.1 Rooms and furniture; prepositions of place

A Label the rooms (a–e) with the words in the box.

bathroom   bedroom   dining room   kitchen   living room

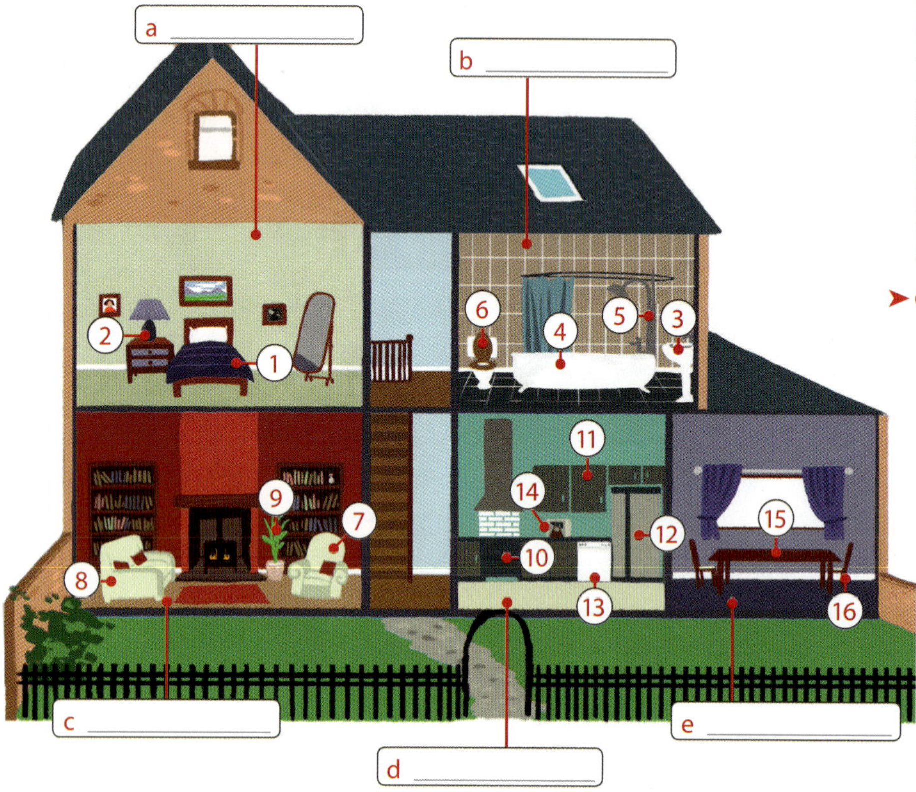

B Look at the picture again. Number the words 1–16.

___ armchair	___ lamp
___ bathtub	___ plant
___ bed	___ shower
___ chair	___ sink
___ coffee machine	___ couch
___ oven	___ table
___ cupboard	___ toilet
___ fridge	___ dishwasher

➤ Go back to page 42.

5.2 Places in a town or city

Match photos (1–12) with the places.

___ café   ___ movie theater   ___ gym   ___ hospital   ___ library   ___ market   ___ museum
___ park   ___ restaurant   ___ grocery store   ___ theater   ___ subway station

➤ Go back to page 44.

2.1 Student A

A Read about another famous family. Answer Student B's questions about the family.

B Ask Student B questions about a famous family. Write the answers.

1 What's his name? ______________

2 What is his dad's name? ______________

3 What is his sister's name? ______________

4 Why are they famous? ______________

➤ Go back to page 13.

2.2 Student A and B

Student A – look at the photos. Choose one person and describe them to your partner.
Student B – listen and guess who your partner is describing.
Then switch roles.

➤ Go back to page 15.

2.1 Student B

A Ask Student A questions about a famous family. Write the answers.

1 What's her first name? ______________________

2 Where is she from? ______________________

3 What are her parents' names? ______________________

4 Why is she famous? ______________________

B Read about another famous family. Answer Student A's questions about the family.

Matthew Centrowitz Jr.

Matthew Centrowitz Jr. is an Olympic athlete from the US. In 2016, he won a gold medal for the 1,500 meters. His father, Matt Centrowitz Sr., is also an Olympic athlete who won a gold medal in the 1979 Pan-American games. Matthew Centrowitz Jr.'s sister Lauren Centrowitz, is also an athlete.

➤ Go back to page 13.

6.1 Student A and B

A **SPEAK** Work in pairs. Read the *City Guide* and choose one thing to do together on the weekend. Explain what you like and don't like to help you decide.

A: Let's go out this weekend!
B: Good idea. What's going on?
A: There's a rock concert in the park on Saturday.
B: Oh, I don't like rock music. Let's go to a nightclub. I love dancing.
A: Sorry, I'm a terrible dancer!

B **SPEAK** Take a class vote. Which events are popular?

➤ Go back to page 53.

City Guide

Movies

French Film Festival ★★★

A festival of French movies, with famous movies like *Amélie*, *That Man from Rio* and *Two Days in Paris*.

Art

Van Gogh – the last years ★★★★★

An exhibit of Van Gogh's paintings from 1888 to 1890.

Clubs

70s disco ★★★★

The 70s disco craze continues. Dance all night to your favorite tunes!

5.3 Student A and B

DISCUSS Work in pairs. Answer the questions about buildings (1–6). Use the adjectives in the box to help you.

1 Describe the buildings.
2 What happens inside?
3 Which building is your favorite? Why?
4 Which building don't you like? Why?

amazing beautiful big boring cool interesting funny modern old small strange tall terrible ugly

➤ Go back to page 47.

W– capital letters

A Look at the visitor card. Where would you fill in a card like this?

a At a university
b On a plane
c At work

B Complete the visitor card with the words in the box.

07713 8765543 1997 10 months Poland ~~Polish~~ student

Visitor card

Last name: Kowalska
First/middle name(s): Marta Irena
Nationality: Polish
Date of birth: month 0 3 day 1 0 year _ _ _ _
Country of birth: ______
Occupation: ______
Passport number: ZS 0067389
Address in the UK: 24 Bridge Street, Leeds, LS5 7RT
Email: mkowalska23@polemail.com
Phone number: ______
What is the main reason for your visit?
business / tourism / (other)
I am here to take a course at a university in Leeds.
Duration of visit: ______

C Complete the rules in the box with words from the visitor card in Exercise B.

Capital letters

You use capital letters for:

- the names of countries Poland
- the names of towns and cities ______
- nationalities ______
- people's names ______
- the personal pronoun 'I' ______

D Look at the student registration form. Find and correct five mistakes with capital letters.

Student registration

Last name: puente
First/middle name(s): Ricardo
Nationality: mexican
Date of birth: month 0 2 day 1 7 year 1 9 9 7
Country of birth: us
Occupation: student
Address in the UK: 11 Lark Close, london, SW5 9JT
Email: m.puente@hotmail.com
Phone number: 07665 456829
What is the main reason for studying English?
business / tourism / (other)
i want to study at a university in the UK.
Duration of visit: 2 weeks

WRITING

Imagine you are on a plane. Complete the visitor card. Remember to use capital letters correctly.

Visitor card

Last name: ______
First/middle name(s): ______
Nationality: ______
Date of birth: month _ _ day _ _ year _ _ _ _
Country of birth: ______
Occupation: ______
Passport number: _ _ _ _ _ _ _ _
Address in the UK: ______
Email: ______
Phone number: _ _ _ _ _ _ _ _ _ _ _
What is the main reason for your visit?
business / tourism / (other)
I am here to take a course at Leeds University.
Duration of visit: ______

2 Writing

Write an email to a friend

W *and*, *but* and *or*

A Read the email. Who is it to?

a a close friend **b** an old friend **c** a colleague

How's things?
Sent: Friday, November 10, 2017, 2:19 pm
To: jbloggs@screen.nett
From: Aiden_28@logbox.com

Hi Joe,

How are you? Long time no see!

How are things? I live in London now with my girlfriend. Do you still live here? How's your family?

Look forward to hearing your news!

Best wishes,

Aiden

B Check (✓) the topics you think Joe will write about in his reply. Then read and check.

- food ☐
- family ☐
- job / school ☐
- friends ☐
- home ☐
- clothes ☐

RE: How's things?
Sent: Friday, November 10, 2017, 4:37 pm
To: Aiden_28@logbox.com
From: jbloggs@screen.nett

Hi Aiden,

I'm very well, thanks. It's great to hear from you!

Yes, we are still in London, but we're not in the apartment anymore. We live in a house because … we have two beautiful children now!

We have a son, Ben, and a daughter, Maya. Ben is three and Maya is four - it's a noisy house! Ben looks like his mom (lucky him!) but he has my personality. He isn't neat or serious, but he's only three! Maya has blond hair and blue eyes like me. Here's a picture for you of all of us on vacation this year!

How about you, Aiden? How are things with you and your family?

Best wishes,

Joe

C Read the email in Exercise B again and underline examples of *and*, *but* and *or*.

D WORK IT OUT Choose the correct words to complete the rules.

and, *but* and *or*

1 We use ***and / but / or*** when we want to add more or similar information in positive statements.
2 We use ***and / but / or*** when we want to add more or similar information in negative statements.
3 We use ***and / but / or*** when we want to add different or unexpected information.

E Complete the sentences with *and*, *or*, or *but*.

1 I have two pets, a cat ______________ a dog.
2 I don't have any children ______________ pets!
3 I live in a house with my friends Amy ______________ Emma.
4 I have a horrible roommate. She isn't friendly ______________ neat!
5 My roommate loves soccer ______________ I hate it.

F SPEAK Work in pairs. Look at the emails in Exercises A and B and answer the questions.

1 How do you start an email to a friend?
2 How do you end an email to a friend?
3 Which phrases are useful when it's the first contact in many months or years?

WRITING

A PLAN Imagine you are responding to the email in Exercise A. Write notes about:

How to start the email
How to answer the questions
How to finish the email.

B WRITE Write your email. Use the email in Exercise B to help you. Remember to:

Start and end your email appropriately
Answer the questions
Use *and*, *but* or *or* to join sentences together.

W– sequencing words

A Work in pairs. Look at the photo in the blog post. Guess the answers to the questions. Explain your ideas.

1 Where's she from?
2 What's her job?
3 Why is she famous?

A DAY in the LIFE of…

about | archive | contact

Ciara Everard Irish 800m champion

January 7, 2017 | Leave a comment

I'm an athlete. On weekdays, I always get up at 8 am. First, I go for a run. I'm usually out for 30 minutes – not long. Then I go home, take a shower and have breakfast – banana pancakes and a cup of tea. I'm not a morning person, so I usually need some coffee, too!

From 10 am to lunchtime, I'm in the gym. I don't like it, but I know it's good for me! After that, I go home and make lunch. I usually have an omelette, some fish and toast. In the afternoon, I'm always really tired, so I sleep for about 30 minutes. At 3 pm, I get up, read my emails and do some work.

At 5 pm, I go for my evening run. Then I exercise and take an ice-bath. At 7 pm, I go home and make dinner. I usually prepare my meals on the weekend so I don't need to cook every night.

In the evening, I relax and watch TV. Finally, I have a snack and go to bed at 11 pm.

B Read the blog post and check your answers to Exercise A.

C Read the blog post again. Complete Ciara's diary.

Day	Time	What?
Mon 26th	8:00 am	*get up and go for a run*
	8:30 am	________
	10:00 am	________
	1:00 pm	________
	2:30 pm	________
	5:00 pm	________
	7:00 pm	________
	11:00 pm	________

D Work in pairs. Would you like a life like Ciara's? Why/Why not?

E Read the first sentence in the box. Then find and underline five sequencing words in the blog post about Ciara Everard.

Sequencing words

We use sequencing words (*first*, *after that*, *then* and *finally*) to help the reader understand the order of things in a text.

- We use [1] ________ to say what we do first.
- We use [2] ________ or [3] ________ to say what we do after another thing.
- We use [4] ________ to say what we do last.

F Complete the rules in the box with the sequencing words you underlined in Exercise E.

WRITING

A PREPARE You are going to write a blog post about your day. Write a diary like Ciara's. Include 6–10 activities you do in a normal day and the times you do them.

B WRITE Use your diary to write a short blog post about your day. Add details and use sequencing words (*first*, *after that*, *then* and *finally*) to explain the order.

C REVIEW Work in pairs. Compare your blog posts.

4 Writing

Write an email asking for information

W – punctuation: question marks, commas and periods

A Work in pairs. Complete the advertisements with the words in the box.

weekend company ten-week course

Start up your own [1] ________

One-day training course with experienced business teacher

Contact Trevor East: teast@ivory.nett

[2] ________ **language courses**

Are you interested in languages?
Learn with us.
Don't wait – call now to get started.
Alena Chin: alenac@onthewall.com

Summer computer skills [3] ________

Do you want to learn computer skills?
Classes every day.
Contact Ed Soames: edso@screen.nett

[4] ________ **résumé writing course**

Five-week course (Saturdays and Sundays only)
Perfect for graduates or people who want to change jobs
Contact Anne Roberts: anne@roberts.nett

B Read the email. Which advertisement is it for?

Inquiry about your course
Sent: Friday, November 10, 2017, 2:19 pm
To: edso@screen.nett
From: SKhan@logbox.com

Dear Mr. Soames,

I am writing to ask about your summer computer skills course.

First, what are the dates of the course? I am free in May, June and July and the first part of August. Second, when do the classes start – are they in the morning or in the afternoon? And finally, how much does the course cost?

I look forward to hearing from you.

Regards,

Samira Khan

C Look at the email in Exercise B again. Circle question marks, commas and periods.

D Look at the question marks, commas and periods that you circled in the email. Choose the correct options to complete the rules.

Punctuation: question marks, commas and full stops

We use *question marks / commas / periods* at the end of sentences.

We use *question marks / commas / periods* at the end of questions.

We use *question marks / commas / periods* to separate words in a list or after sequencing words.

E Number the stages of the email in Exercise B.

___ Asking about when the course starts and ends
_1_ Greeting and name of the person you're writing to
___ Standard 'end of letter' phrase
___ Reason for writing
___ Asking about the times of classes
___ Salutation and name of writer
___ Asking about the cost of the course

F Complete the table with the phrases in the box.

All the best Best wishes Dear Monica Dear Mr. Ikeda ~~Dear Mrs. Bennett~~ Kind regards ~~Sincerely yours~~

Starting an email	Finishing an email
Dear Mrs. Bennett	Sincerely yours

G Order the two groups of phrases in Exercise F from most formal to least formal.

WRITING

A PREPARE Imagine you want to apply to one of the courses in Exercise A. Choose a course and write three questions to ask in an email.

B WRITE Write an email asking for information. Use the email in Exercise B to help you.

C REVIEW Work in pairs. Check your partner's email for:

- spelling and punctuation
- grammar
- organization

5 Writing

Write a description of a place

W – using adjectives

A Work in pairs. Look at the picture in the review. Answer the questions.

1 What can you see? Describe the building.
2 What do you think this building is?
3 Where do you think it is?

B Read the online review. Check your answers to questions 2 and 3 in Exercise A.

C Read the review again. Choose the correct answers a, b or c.

1 What is the Villa Borghese?
  a a museum
  b a park
  c a café
2 What can you see in the museum?
  a paintings and furniture
  b cars and transportation
  c furniture and clothes
3 Why does the writer like the café?
  a because it's warm inside
  b because it's popular
  c because the food is good

D Read again. Underline the adjectives that the writer uses to describe these things:

- the park
- the paintings
- the museum building
- the rooms in the museum
- the sandwiches

Using adjectives

When you write, use a variety of adjectives to make your writing more interesting.

*Villa Borghese is a **famous** park in Rome. It's very **big** and it's **beautiful**.*

Villa Borghese is a famous park in **Rome**. It's very big and it's beautiful. It's a great place to spend a couple of hours.

There's a museum in the park, the Borghese Gallery. There are some amazing paintings in the museum. The building is very interesting, too. It's an old, white house with a lot of windows. Inside the house, the rooms are beautiful. They have some old furniture in them.

There's a café inside the gallery, but I like the café in the park. It's very popular. You can sit outside and have lunch under the trees. The sandwiches are delicious!

Share Like Comment

E Read about the Eiffel Tower. Change the adjectives *nice* and *good* for more interesting adjectives.

The Eiffel Tower is a nice tower in Paris, France. It's very popular with tourists. It's a nice place to spend an hour. It's tall and it's a very nice shape. There aren't any windows, and there aren't any walls. It's gray. I think it's really nice. You can go to the top of the Eiffel Tower. The views of the city are good. There's a restaurant on the first floor. The food is good.

WRITING

A PREPARE Choose a building, place or landmark in your city (or in a city that you know well). Think about these questions:

1 What is the building?
2 Where is it?
3 What does it look like?
4 What is your opinion of it?
5 What can you see and do there?
6 Can you eat or drink anything there?

B PLAN Think about your answers in Exercise A. What adjectives can you use to describe topics 1–6 in Exercise A?

C WRITE Write your description. Use a variety of adjectives to make your writing more interesting.

Write a review of an event

using narrative sequencers

A Work in pairs. Look at the picture. What do you think happens at this event?

B Read the review. Check your answer to Exercise A.

C Choose the correct words to complete the sentences.

According to the review, …

1 the tour leader was *funny* / *serious*.
2 the tourists *learned* / *didn't learn* about Melbourne.
3 it lasted for *30 minutes* / *60 minutes*.
4 the weather was *good* / *bad*.
5 it was *cheap* / *expensive*.
6 it was a *good* / *bad* experience.

D Read the review again. Number the topics 1–6 in the order they are written about.

___ The weather
___ The location
_1_ The type of event
___ The writer's opinion
___ The cost of the event
___ Details of the event

E Look back at the review. Underline the narrative sequencers. Use the information in the box to help you.

Using narrative sequencers

- To begin the story, we use *first* or *to start with*.
  First, we met in the city center.
  To start with, we got some headphones.
- To continue the story, we use *then*, *next* and *after that*.
  Then, we went to Main Street.
  Next, we learned about the city.
  After that, we had lunch.
- To end the story, we use *finally* or *in the end*.
  Finally, the concert ended.
  In the end, we called a taxi.

F Complete the story with narrative sequencers. Use the information in the box to help you.

Last weekend was really busy. Saturday evening was Comedy Night at The Old Fire Station. [1]_______________, we watched a comedian – I can't remember his name. [2]_______________, we saw the famous Ali Wong. She was great. We laughed a lot! [3]_______________, there was a band for about 45 minutes. [4]_______________, the evening ended with a routine by Kyle Kinane. He was very funny, too. It was a great evening's entertainment and excellent value – it cost $30 each.

WRITING

A PREPARE You're going to write a review for an event you went to. Think about the event and write notes under the headings in Exercise D.

B WRITE Use your notes to write your review. Use narrative sequencers to help you organize your ideas.

Guru Dudu Silent Disco Walking Tour

★★★★

goodreviews, January 18, 2018

I went to my first disco 20 years ago. I went to my first silent disco last week. Well, my first silent disco walking tour!

The tour started outside the Federation Square in Melbourne. First, we each got some wireless headphones and followed Guru Dudu, our tour leader and DJ, through the streets of the city. Then, we met some local people who talked about the history of the city. After that, we walked, danced and laughed as Guru Dudu played dance music and made jokes through our headphones. It was a great way to see the city. It was warm and sunny, and everyone had fun. Finally, the tour ended back where it started. The whole thing lasted an hour. It really was the best city tour ever! And it was a great value at just $24 a ticket. I really recommend it!

Reviewed by Tom

Irregular Verbs

Infinitive	Past simple	Past participle
be	was/were	been
become	became	become
begin	began	begun
break	broke	broken
bring	brought	brought
build	built	built
buy	bought	bought
can	could	(been able to)
catch	caught	caught
choose	chose	chosen
come	came	come
cost	cost	cost
cut	cut	cut
do	did	done
drink	drank	drunk
eat	ate	eaten
fall	fell	fallen
feel	felt	felt
find	found	found
forget	forgot	forgotten
get	got	got
give	gave	given
go	went	gone/been
grow	grew	grown
have	had	had
hear	heard	heard
hit	hit	hit
hold	held	held
hurt	hurt	hurt
keep	kept	kept
know	knew	known
leave	left	left
lend	lent	lent

Infinitive	Past simple	Past participle
let	let	let
lose	lost	lost
make	made	made
mean	meant	meant
meet	met	met
must	had to	(had to)
pay	paid	paid
put	put	put
read	read	read
ride	rode	ridden
run	ran	run
say	said	said
see	saw	seen
sell	sold	sold
set	set	set
shut	shut	shut
sing	sang	sung
sit	sat	sat
sleep	slept	slept
speak	spoke	spoken
spell	spelled	spelled
spend	spent	spent
stand	stood	stood
steal	stole	stolen
take	took	taken
teach	taught	taught
tell	told	told
think	thought	thought
throw	threw	thrown
understand	understood	understood
wear	wore	worn
win	won	won
write	wrote	written

PHONETIC SYMBOLS

Single vowels			Diphthongs			Consonants					
/ɪ/	fi**sh**	/fɪʃ/	/ɪə/	**ear**	/ɪə/	/p/	**p**en	/pen/	/s/	**s**nake	/sneɪk/
/iː/	b**ea**n	/biːn/	/eɪ/	f**a**ce	/feɪs/	/b/	**b**ag	/bæg/	/z/	**z**oo	/zuː/
/ʊ/	f**oo**t	/fʊt/	/ʊə/	t**ou**rist	/'tʊərɪst/	/t/	**t**ea	/tiː/	/ʃ/	**sh**op	/ʃɒp/
/uː/	sh**oe**	/ʃuː/	/ɔɪ/	b**oy**	/bɔɪ/	/d/	**d**og	/dɒg/	/ʒ/	televi**si**on	/'telɪvɪʒən/
/e/	**e**gg	/eg/	/əʊ/	n**o**se	/nəʊz/	/ʧ/	**ch**ip	/ʧɪp/	/m/	**m**ap	/mæp/
/ə/	moth**er**	/'mʌðə/	/ju/	**u**se	/juz/	/ʤ/	**j**azz	/ʤæz/	/n/	**n**ame	/neɪm/
/ɜː/	w**or**d	/wɜːd/	/aɪ/	**eye**	/aɪ/	/k/	**c**ake	/keɪk/	/ŋ/	ri**ng**	/rɪŋ/
/ɔː/	t**a**lk	/tɔːk/	/aʊ/	m**ou**th	/maʊθ/	/g/	**g**irl	/gɜːl/	/h/	**h**ouse	/haʊs/
/æ/	b**a**ck	/bæk/				/f/	**f**ilm	/fɪlm/	/l/	**l**eg	/leg/
/ʌ/	b**u**s	/bʌs/				/v/	**v**erb	/vɜːb/	/r/	**r**oad	/rəʊd/
/ɑː/	**ar**m	/ɑːm/				/θ/	**th**ing	/θɪŋ/	/w/	**w**ant	/wɒnt/
/ɒ/	t**o**p	/tɒp/				/ð/	**th**ese	/ðiːz/	/j/	**y**es	/jes/

Audio scripts

UNIT 1

Lesson 1.1, Listening, Exercise A

1.1 **H = Helen V = Veronica P = Pilot**

H: Excuse me, is this row 15?

V: Yes. I'm in seat 15A.

H: My seat is 15B. Hi, I'm Helen.

V: Nice to meet you. I'm Veronica Martinez.

H: That's a nice name. I like Spanish names.

V: Thanks, but I'm not Spanish. I'm Mexican. I'm from Mexico. Where are you from?

H: I'm Canadian, but I live in Mexico. My company's office is in Mexico City.

P: Good morning, ladies and gentlemen. This is the 9:45 flight to Mexico City …

Lesson 1.2, Listening, Exercise A

1.9 **L = Lee C = Carlos**

L: Hello?

C: Hi, Lee, it's Carlos. Where are you? Are you still in Tokyo?

L: Oh, hi, Carlos! No, I'm not. I'm 1,300 miles from Tokyo. I'm in China now.

C: Wow! Where are you in China?

L: I'm in Beijing.

C: Cool. What's it like there?

L: It's very busy in the center. There are lots of new buildings and long streets. It's a big city.

C: Is the food good?

L: Yes, it is. I really like Chinese food.

C: What's your next destination?

L: I don't know. Maybe Shanghai, or maybe the countryside.

C: Sounds fun! Send me more photos!

L: I will!

Lesson 1.3, Listening, Exercise B

1.10 **N = Narrator G = Guard W = Woman M = Man**

N: 1

G: Excuse me, ma'am. Is this your bag?

W: Yes, it is.

G: I need to look inside. Oh, is this a bottle of water?

W: Yes, it is.

G: Sorry, bottles aren't allowed.

W: Oh, of course. I'm sorry.

G: Is there a laptop or a phone in this bag?

W: No, there isn't.

G: OK. You can go. Oh, wait! Are these your keys?

W: Oh, yes, they are. Thank you so much!

N: 2

G: Excuse me, sir. Is that your bag?

M: Yes, it is.

G: Can you bring it here, please?

M: Sure.

G: Is your phone in this bag?

M: Yes, it is.

G: You need to take it out, please.

M: Oh, OK.

G: Thank you … One more thing …

M: Yes?

G: Are those your bags?

M: No, they aren't. I think they belong to that family over there.

G: I see. You can go.

UNIT 2

Lesson 2.2, Listening, Exercise B

2.5 **W = Woman**

W: My brother doesn't look like me. We both have long red hair, but everything else is different. He's short, and I'm not. I'm very slim, but he isn't. He has glasses. I don't. And he has a beard. I definitely don't have a beard.

Lesson 2.3, Listening, Exercise A

2.7 **F = Fiona K = Keisha**

F: I like this picture.

K: This is on our first day. These are the people in my study group.

F: Everyone looks so happy.

K: Yes. They're all really friendly and nice.

F: That's great! So, who is who?

K: The girl with dark, curly hair is Zoe. She's my best friend. She's a very funny person.

F: Are any of your roommates in this picture?

K: Yes! Jody is my roommate. She has long hair.

F: Does she have black hair?

K: No, that's Alice. She's fairly quiet, but I like her. This is Jody – she has long, blond hair.

F: Is she neat? It's good to have neat roommates.

K: Yes, she is. She's fairly serious and very neat! I'm the messy one in our apartment!

UNIT 3

Lesson 3.1, Listening, Exercise B

3.1 **T = Tom V = Venus**

T: Hello, and welcome to *Two minutes* with me, Tom Fenn. Our guest today is Venus Mack, who is phoning in from California. Good morning, Venus.

V: Hey, Tom. Hey, UK. Good evening from Los Angeles.

T: You have two minutes to tell us about your typical day.

V: OK, well, my name's Venus Mack, I'm 25 years old and I'm a late night DJ for a radio station here in L.A.! I live in a small house, and – uh – a typical day? My day is unusual because I get up at four o'clock in the afternoon. That's right! Four pm. So, first, I go for a long run. My dog, Bowie, comes, too. Then, I go home, take a shower and have breakfast – breakfast at 6 pm, right? – it's usually fruit and coffee. I leave home at around 6:30. I go to work by car. Everyone drives here in L.A.! I get to work at 8 pm. I love my job! I meet a lot of musicians, and some of them are on my show. This week it's a band – from the UK – called Reuben. My show starts at 10 pm and ends at 2 am. After the show, I work with my producer, Joel, and prepare for the next show. I finish work at 6 am and then I go to a café and have coffee with friends, and maybe some dinner, and then I go home to give Bowie his breakfast. I go to bed at around 9 am.

T: Fantastic! Thanks, Venus.

Lesson 3.2, Listening, Exercise B

3.4 **I = Ian A = Ali**

I: So, are you ready for screen-free week, Ali?

A: Screen what?

Audio scripts

I: Screen-free week. No internet, no cell phone, no TV for a week.

A: What? You're joking!

I: Ali, how many hours a day are you on your phone?

A: How many hours a day? I don't know. About nine? From early in the morning to late at night.

I: You look at it when you wake up?

A: Yeah, my phone is my alarm clock! Then, I look at the news and read my texts and emails.

I: What about during the day, at work?

A: Well, I use maps on my phone all the time for work. I have an app. It's great! It tells me if there are problems on the roads.

I: What about after work?

A: Yeah, I use my phone a lot in the evening – I talk to my friends – well, *text* my friends or play games with them online. On the weekend, we watch soccer on TV, and we chat online – we have a group chat – about the games. On Saturday and Sunday, it's non-stop soccer! I love soccer!

I: So, what about screen-free week?

A: No way! Impossible! I need my phone!

Lesson 3.3, Listening, Exercise A
3.9 **C = Carlos M = Moira**

C: Moira, are you free tomorrow night?

M: I don't know. Why?

C: Well, tomorrow is September 16th – Independence Day in my country – and there's a party at my friend's house. Do you want to come?

M: Oh, that sounds like fun! I'd love to come. We have Independence Day in my country, too. How do you celebrate it in Mexico?

C: All the stores and banks close and everyone takes a day off because it's party time! There are parties everywhere. People play music in the streets. Everybody dances and sings.

M: Oh, it's the same in Madagascar. We all dance and sing in the streets, too. There's usually a big parade in town – and we eat special food!

C: In Mexico, there's a big parade in Mexico City, and in the evening, we go and watch the fireworks! It's really noisy!

M: Oh, I love fireworks!

C: And we put up red, white and green decorations. That's the color of our flag.

M: Madagascar's flag is red, white and green, too! We don't put up decorations, but we wear traditional clothes and dance … and sing …

C: We don't wear traditional clothes, but we shout 'Viva Mexico!' and we dance!

M: I want to go to Mexico next September!

C: Well, come to the party tomorrow and it will be just like Mexico!

UNIT 4

Lesson 4.2, Listening, Exercise A
4.5 **S = Salah H = Hussam**

S: How's your new job?

H: It's great. I don't have to work nine to five. I can choose my own hours.

S: That's great, so when do you work?

H: I usually start work at noon. Why? When do *you* start?

S: I start really early in the morning. Sometimes before six!

H: Ugh! I couldn't do that!! I usually take it easy in the morning because I don't go to bed until midnight or later.

S: When do you have lunch?

H: I have lunch any time I feel like it. Some days, I have lunch at 1 pm, other days I eat late in the afternoon.

S: What time do you usually finish work?

H: I finish when I want to. I don't have to ask my boss. It's my decision.

S: That's amazing. So you can leave whenever you like?

H: No, I don't leave. I stay where I am.

S: I don't understand.

H: I don't work in an office. I'm self-employed now. I work from home.

Lesson 4.3, Listening, Exercise A
4.7 **T = Tom L = Lily**

T: Hello. Can I help you?

L: Hi. Yes, please. I work in an office, but I want to change jobs. I'd like to take a course.

T: Well, you've come to the right place. We offer over 800 courses. My name's Tom. Come and sit down.

L: Thank you. I'm Lily.

T: Nice to meet you, Lily. Now, what subject do you want to study?

L: I want to train to be a teacher.

T: Ah, an excellent job! We have a very good teacher training course. I'm a teacher myself.

L: Oh?

T: Yes, I teach an art history course and …

L: I want to teach art history!

T: That's great! I can definitely help you.

L: Do I have to go to a university?

T: Yes, you do.

L: That's a problem. I have to stay at work while I study. I need the money.

T: I recommend online classes. You study when you want. You work from home and you send your homework to us by email.

L: That sounds good. I want to get a certification. Does this course offer one?

T: Yes, of course! This is a degree course. You pay for access to our online materials and we provide you with your own teacher. The teacher of this art history course is … um, well … me actually.

L: Oh! OK!

T: At the end of each course, you take an exam. You can pay for one year at first and see how you like it. Then, after two more years, you can get a degree.

L: That sounds great. Now, how much …

UNIT 5

Lesson 5.1, Listening, Exercise C
5.4 **S = Sadie L = Luke**

S: Hello? Is this Luke Westman?

L: This is Luke speaking.

S: My name's Sadie Parfitt. I'm calling about your beach house.

L: Sure! Where are you from?

S: I'm from the south of England.

L: OK, that's great.

S: Uh … yes. So, are there any beds in your house?

L: Beds? Yes, there are. There are two beds. There's a bed in the bedroom and another bed across from the kitchen.

S: Very good. And is there an oven?

L: Yes, there's an oven. It's in the kitchen. There's a fridge, a coffee machine and a dishwasher, too.

S: I see. Is there a swimming pool?

L: Yeah, sure there is. It's huge … It's called the Pacific Ocean!

S: Sorry? There is a swimming pool?

L: No, ma'am. It's a joke. It's the ocean. No, there isn't a swimming pool.

S: Oh! Yes, a joke. Great. So, is there a yard?

L: A yard? No, there isn't a yard – there's a beach. It's a caravan by the beach.

S: A caravan? The advertisement said a 'wonderful home' …

L: It *is* a wonderful home!

S: OK … Well, are there any chairs in the dining room?

L: No, there aren't any chairs. It's a dining area, not a dining room. There's a table, and four people can sit at the table, but there aren't any chairs.

S: I see.

L: So, tell me about your house. How many bedrooms are there?

S: My house? Oh, I don't have a house.

L: But … this is a house swap. We swap houses. You stay in my house and I stay in your house …

S: No, sorry, I don't have a house. So when can I stay in your caravan?

L: OK, ma'am. Thank you for calling. Goodbye now. Thanks.

UNIT 6

6.4 Lesson 6.2, Listening, Exercise B

G = Grandad C = Carrie

G: Hey, Carrie. Let's watch that new nature show on TV. It starts in five minutes.

C: Oh, I can't, Grandpa. Mom says I have to do my homework. But we can watch it later.

G: Later? It ends at seven.

C: I can get it on demand. We can watch it on my tablet.

G: On demand?

C: Yeah. You know, you don't have to watch TV shows at a specific time on TV any more. You can watch them online, whenever you like.

G: So, can I watch the soccer game from yesterday?

C: Yes! You know, most people watch TV on demand now. Last night, I watched three episodes of my favorite TV show.

G: Amazing! When I was young, my favorite TV show was on once a week. On Tuesday nights. It was a music show.

C: How many TV channels were there?

G: Hmm … There weren't many TV channels. Three, I think.

C: Three? Now there are hundreds. Was it boring?

G: No, it wasn't.

C: Were TVs cheap back then?

G: No, they weren't. They were expensive. TV wasn't an everyday thing. We were the first family on our street to get one. It was in 1951, when I was ten. That's nearly 70 years ago! TV was special in the 1950s. We all watched TV together – the whole family. It was the same in every home in the country.

C: Everyone at the same time? That's funny. Were they happy?

G: Yes, they were. It was normal!

C: Mom and Dad often watch TV on their laptops and Susan has a tablet. We all watch TV alone.

G: People today spend more time alone. It was very different when I was young. Parents, children, grandparents were all together more. TV was a shared experience.

C: Was that nice, Grandpa?

G: Yes, it was. I wasn't lonely. People did things together. It was fun.

Notes

Macmillan Education
4 Crinan Street
London N1 9XW
A division of Macmillan Education Limited

Companies and representatives throughout the world

American Language Hub Level 1A Student's Book ISBN 978-1-380-04692-5
American Language Hub Level 1A Student's Book with Student's App
ISBN 978-1-380-04686-4

Text, design and illustration © Macmillan Education Limited 2020
Written by Peter Maggs and Catherine Smith

With thanks to Edward Price and Carol Goodwright for additional authoring and to Signature Manuscripts for the Grammar Hub pages.

The authors have asserted their right to be identified as the authors of this work in accordance with the Copyright, Designs and Patents Act 1988.

The right of Sue Kay and Vaughan Jones to be identified as authors of the Speaking Pages in this work has been asserted by them in accordance with the Copyright, Designs and Patents Act 1988.

First published 2020

All rights reserved. No part of this publication may be reproduced, stored in a retrieval system, or transmitted in any form or by any means, electronic, mechanical, photocopying, recording, or otherwise, without the prior written permission of the publishers.

Designed by emc design ltd
Illustrated by Rasmus Juul, Rose Frith represented by Lemonade Illustration Agency, Peter Lubach (Beehive illustration)
Cover design by Restless
Cover image by Plainpicture/Cultura/dotdotred
Picture research by Emily Taylor
Café Hub videos produced by Creative Listening
Café Hub video scripts written by James and Luke Vyner

The authors and publishers would like to thank the following for permission to reproduce their photographs:

Alamy Dominic Dibbs pXXIX, ImageBROKER p43(bl), Rosalrene Betancourt p44(bl), Theatrepix p56(tl); **Steve Cole** p17(cr); **Comstock Images** p58-59(background); **Getty Images** pp12(tr), 27(party), 28-29(background), 33(4), XIX(3.1.1), XIX(3.1.2), XIX(3.1.5), XIX(3.1.6), XIX(4.1.4), XIX(4.1.7), XX(5), XX(6), XXI(2.2.1, 2.2.5, 2.2.6), Aga fotostock pXIX(4.1.6), ArcaidImages pp47(4), 50, Archive Photos Creative p54(3), Yuri Arcurs pXX(1), Petri Artturi Asikainen pp21, Aurora Creative p33(3), Liam Bailey p31, Thomas Barwick pp34(tl), Markus Bernhard p17(bcr), Bildagentur p47(5), Phil Boorman pXXVII, Caiaimage/Paul Bradbury p35(1), Brand New Images pp24(topdog), 59(br), BraunS p24(tr), James Brittain p52(2), Gary Burchell p113, Peter Burnett p106, Caiaimage pp16, 22(tr), 34(tr), 54(4), Ramsey Cardy pXXII, Cescassawin p46(1), Christopherarndt p44(tl), Stewart Cohen p2(tl), Cultura pp33(1), Jake Curtis pp24(tl), Datacraft Co Ltd p5(2), Nick David pVI(c), Jacques Demarthon p51, Digital Vision ppVI(b), XIX(3.1.3), dj murdok photos p12-13(background), Michael Dodge p56(tr), Dorling Kindersley pp7(saw), Richard Drury p24(lisab), E+ ppVI(a), 7(water), 42(bl), Johannes Eisele pp26(tr), Eric Raptosh Photography p17(t), EyeEm pp3(b), 8-9(background), 24(tl), 38-39(background), FangXiaNuo pXX(4), FoodPix p18(Croissant), Marvin Fox p3(tl), Tony C French pp15(r), 22(tl), Baptiste Giroudon p52(3), Steve Glass p25(br), GoodLifeStudio pXIX(4.1.1), Dennis Hallinan p54(1), Hero Images XX(2), Gary Houlder pXIX(4.1.8), Hulton Archive Creative p54(2), The Image Bank pp27(balinese dancers), XX(3), iStockphoto pXX(9, 10), XXVIII, Jetta Productions p35(2), JGI/Jamie Grill p23, J J D p14(1), Joegolby p53, John Warburton-Lee Photography p27(parade), Johner RF p52(4), Jupiterimages p27(card), Steve Kelley p27(fireworks), Barry King p12(bl), KingWu p5(3), Thomas Kurmeier pXXIII (5.3.1), Kyoshino p18-19(background), Lonely Planet Images pp45, LOOK pXXIII (5.3.2), Macduff Everton/Botanica p15(l), Megan Maloy pXIX(3.1.9), Daniel MacDonald pXXI (2.2.2), Irina Marwan p26(br), Maskot pXXI (2.2.7), Miss Passion Photography p41, Dean Mitchell p151(12), Momo productions p24(milos), Tara Moore pp17(br), m.p.imageart pXXI (2.2.3), Peter Muller p24(celine), National Geographic ppXX(7), Nikada p5(1), Liam Norris pXIX(3.1.7), OJO p33(2), Gabriel Olsen p12(br), Photonica p42(tr), Pixdeluxe p7(b), Pixland pXXV, Martin Putty p1, Presley Ann p12(bm), Redferns pXXI, Robert Harding World Imagery pp11, Selimaksan p55, Stone Sub p52(5), Tadamasa Taniguchi p24(fumi), Tetra images pXXI (2.2.8), Alys Tomlinson p52(6), Universal Images Group pp2(map), 52(1), XVIII (maps), Universal Images Group pXXIII (5.3.6), Klaus Vedfelt pp14(2), 37, Vetta pp36, Mark Viker p7(toiletries), Visit Britain pXX(12), Visual China Group p26(bl), Tom Werner p32, Westend61 pp24(scotgirl), XIX(4.1.3, 4.1.5), XX(11), pXXI (2.2.4), WestLight p39(folders); **ImageSource** pp48-49(background), XIX(4.1.2); **iStockphoto** pp7(phone), 18(camera, phone), 42(br); **Photodisc** pp7(bat), 18(umbrella); **Rex features** Morgan Treacy/INPHO/Shutterstock pXXVI; **Shutterstock** Cesc Assawin pXXI (5.3.3), Kaprik p46(3), Korkusung p4(tl), Felix Lipov pXXIII (5.3.5), Denis Rozhnovsky pXIX (3.1.8), Volha Stasevich pXXIII (5.3.4), StockPhotosArt p46(2), Kirayonak Yuliya p24(tm); **Springer Nature Limited** pp7(keys), 18(keys); **Stockbyte** pp7(scissors); **SWNS Group** p14(a,b); **Thinkstock** pp7(laptop), 18(laptop, headphones, skateboard), XIX(3.1.4), XX(8).

Commissioned photographs in the Café Hubs by Creative Listening.

The authors and publishers are grateful for permission to reprint the following copyright material:

p14 Extract from 'One is dark-skinned and one is white, one has brown eyes and the other blue - but Bobby and Riley are million-to-one TWINS' by Jennifer Newton. Originally published in MailOnline, 5th July 2015. © Associated Newspapers Ltd. Reprinted with permission of Solo Syndication; p36 Extract from The Open University. © The Open University 2018. All Rights Reserved. Reprinted with permission of The Open University; pXXVI Extract from 'A day in the life: Ireland's 800m Olympic hopeful Ciara Everard' by The42 Team. Originally published in The 42, 12th January 2016. Content copyright © Journal Media Ltd. 2018. Reprinted with permission of The 42.

These materials may contain links for third party websites. We have no control over, and are not responsible for, the contents of such third party websites. Please use care when accessing them.

The inclusion of any specific companies, commercial products, trade names or otherwise, does not constitute or imply its endorsement or recommendation by Macmillan Education Limited.

Printed and bound in Mexico
by Compañía Editorial Ultra, S.A. de C.V.

2021 2020
04 03 02 01